Riding the Crocodile, Flying the Peach Pit

A Sensory Approach to Education

Peter Majoy

Zephyr Press®

REACHING THEIR HIGHEST POTENTIAL
Tucson, Arizona

Riding the Crocodile, Flying the Peach Pit
A Sensory Approach to Education

Grades K–12

© 1996 by Zephyr Press
Printed in the United States of America

ISBN 1-56976-038-1

Editors: Stacey Lynn and Stacey Shropshire
Cover design: Stirling Crebbs
Illustrations: Kimmy Su
Design and Production: Daniel Miedaner
Typesetting: Daniel Miedaner

Zephyr Press
P.O. Box 66006
Tucson, AZ 85728-6006

Library of Congress Cataloging-in-Publication Data

Majoy, Peter, 1943-
    Riding the crocodile, flying the peach pit : a sensory approach to education / Peter Majoy.
        p.   cm.
    Includes bibliographical references (p.).
    ISBN 1-56976-038-1
    1. Perceptual learning. 2. Senses and sensation. 3. Learning, Psychology of. 4. Activity programs in education. I. Title.
    LB1067.M334 1996
        370.15'5—dc20   96-22548

For Theresa

*It is when the senses are
fully engaged and challenged
that we fully engage
and challenge the mind.*

Contents

Introduction

Competing for the Senses

Imagine yourself on the scaly, ridged back of a crocodile who is riding a peach pit, flying to somewhere. In this simple suggestion are the seeds for complex interactions between neurons within your whole brain–whole body system. A thousand nights of countless twinkling stars could not compare to the myriad bursts of inner star systems that communicated instantaneously with each other as you imagined this adventure.

On the same crocodile–peach pit ride, fly through an amusement park on a busy day. Hear the screams of children on the roller coaster and the vendors selling cotton candy. Suddenly change venues and fly several feet above the ocean near a whale whose spout is sending spray in all directions. You can hear the movement of the whale and the spraying water. You probably can feel the water as your body responds to the coolness of the spray. Again, your brain dances in a quiet storm of electrical impulses as you forget where you are and enter the suggestion.

Imagine yourself perusing issue 10 of the magazine *Mondo 2000*. On the cover you see an art editor holding a pair of eyeballs. Inside you find ads for computer software for artists, programs in virtual reality, interactive CD-ROMs, an article about Terence McKenna, and myriad ads and articles with a common thread—the cybernetic world of information technology. What has the greatest impact on you are the visuals created by computers in the production of the magazine. This cybernetic cosmos could very effectively deliver the multisensory suggestions given in the preceding two paragraphs. The technology to deliver the experience is here, and it will climax with virtual reality (already being popularized by SEGA).

Keep your imagination in gear. You are sitting back in your favorite chair, about to whisk through Perelman's book *School's Out: Hyperlearning, the New Technology, and the End of Education* (1992). You fixate on the bottom of page 296, where Perelman is attempting to explain how technology is slowly but surely making an objective assessment of possible ability. His line of thought jumps from assessing physical prowess of potential factory workers to assessment of educational ability: "Similar assessment technology either exists or could be developed (with sensible national R&D priorities) to gauge functional abilities across the spectrum of cognitive, interpersonal, and other human intelligences listed by Howard Gardner." You imagine someone trying to assess your experience of riding the crocodile upon the flying peach pit. You feel yourself about to burst out laughing. Alas, no machine is present to assess the quality of your laughter.

Your imagination flies as you reach to a stack of magazines and pick up the summer 1993 *Holistic Education Review*, the theme of which is "Technology and Childhood." The cover picture of a child sitting at a desk playing at a computer catches your eye, but more intriguing is the fact that the setting is a beach and the sand is still wet from the ebbing tide. You are curious. The images of nature and the child in all their fluid unpredictability are set against the logical digitality of the computer. You feel your fingertips turn each page until you come to William Crain's article "Technological Time Values and the Assault on Healthy Development" (1993). You look for the meat you suspect hangs somewhere in the exposition. Yes! There it is: "For the child seated at a computer terminal, there is no paint, sand or water; no grass, wind or bird song. The child is cut off from the rich, sensual experiences that are vital for perceptual and creative development" (29).

You are temporarily relieved to read from Bill Gates's *The Road Ahead* that "Learning with a computer will be a springboard for learning away from the computer. Young children will still need to touch toys and tools with their hands. Seeing chemical reactions on a computer screen can be a good supplement to hands-on work in the chemistry lab, but it can't replace the real experience. Children need personal interaction with each other and with adults to learn social and interpersonal skills, such as how to work cooperatively." Gates goes out of his way to assure you that technology will not replace teachers, but you still remain concerned, wanting to maintain a creative mind that is open to the enormous potential of the computer, the Internet, and the World Wide Web, but you wonder if Gates has truly thought through the real hurdles educators will have to leap over to maintain a sense of senses within schools today. Your mind works at lightning speed. Of course! At least one arena of educational change becomes apparent to you. There is a deepening competition for control of the senses. It is the senses that hold the key to educational reform, for they provide food for the mind.

Your imagination gathers its resources at warp speed and you see several educational scenarios. Your first image is of a teacher taking a group of school children through the crocodile house at the zoo and stopping to eat peaches. You hear the teacher tell the children to save the pits and to be sure to bring them to class the next day. The children will explore their experience through poetry and critical thinking exercises.

The second scenario places the same children and teacher before a large television screen hooked up to a computer with a CD-ROM database that is currently showing a documentary about crocodiles. The kids are eating peaches and saving the pits for the same poetry and critical thinking exercises.

The third scenario involves virtual reality headgear that allows the children to swim with the crocodiles in a perceptual field that seems realistic. Gloves and body suits hooked up to the computer allow the children to feel the crocodiles and the changes in body temperature produced by the water in which they swim. Again, the children take time out for a peach snack and save the pit for later.

You can't help but notice that in this last scenario there is no teacher. The children are engulfed in a web of technology that nurtures and instructs them in their every move. A technology master is visible on a huge screen to give some image of human guidance in the otherwise completely cybernetic environment.

You are deep into imagery and feeling a tension in your body because the imagined scenarios end with sensations that are completely computer generated, totally engaging of the children, and orchestrated by a mediated environment without the need for a teacher. These scenarios bother you. You feel a bit agitated.

At this point you may find yourself thirsting for some direction. You are aloft with the crocodile and the peach pit, but your imagination conjures up a question: in the long run, on what does a child depend for sensory information, and does this dependency require the mediation of a teacher? Crocodiles that fly with aerial peach pits really can't be witnessed firsthand. Either a teacher or media must introduce this stimulus to a student. The source of the image, either teacher or media, is itself a stimulus, a sensory experience with which the crocodile and the peach pit become associated.

On the other hand, direct contact with a crocodile or a peach pit cannot be mediated; it does require human direction, guidance, and interaction. This need for mediation raises a question about education and sensory experience: to what extent do we want education to depend on mediated sensory experience as the basis for contact with nature and the basis for the development of students as writers, artists, and thinkers?

Your bookshelf is coughing at you as if to say you should notice what it has to offer. Mysteriously, a book comes tumbling off the shelf into your lap. It is Zejonc's *Catching the Light: The Entwined History of Light and Mind* (1993). It is open to the page on which the author is explaining Cezanne's penchant for repainting a scene over and over again. To Cezanne, nature was not static. As he stood before a natural setting, it would constantly change. Nature seemed to possess a dynamic life that made Cezanne change each painting until he felt there was a correspondence between his inner eye and the scene before him: "The eye becomes concentric, aligned with nature, through the artist's ceaseless action of looking and working, of struggling to see clearly a single gesture of nature's infinitely varied repertoire, and then to paint it. In guiding the hand across a canvas, one fashions and refines fresh senses, new capacities of mind suited to seeing that which until then had eluded the eye" (339).

There is no doubt that more and more sensory experience is going to be mediated in the world of tomorrow. We must make decisions about a balance between direct contact with nature (including direct contact with flesh-and-blood teachers) and mediated contact through state-of-the-art technology. As Cezanne realized, there is something dynamic in nature itself that refines and teaches the mind new tricks; of course, the medium itself is a valid contact with nature, one that is especially powerful the more sophisticated our technology becomes. Yet there is something lacking in this sophistication; let us call this missing element "technological sensory naivete."

The next book ready to drop from your bookshelf is one that at first glance seems hardly a resource for exploration of the necessary utilization of the senses in whole-brain teaching and learning. But you are pleasantly surprised to find that Wendell Berry's *The Unsettling of American Culture and Agriculture* (1977) gives profound insight into the sensory base of learning. Berry comments on the replacement of the pastoral-agricultural metaphor of life with the metaphor of the machine. Berry avers that the former "preserved in human care, the natural cycles of birth, growth, death, and decay" (56). About the machine culture that we have become, Berry states that "we have eliminated any fear or awe or reverence or humility or delight or joy that might have restrained us in our use of the world. We have indeed learned to act as if our sovereignty were unlimited and as if our intelligence were equal to the universe. Our 'success' is a catastrophic demonstration of our failure. The industrial paradise is a fantasy in the minds of the privileged and the powerful; the reality is a shambles" (56).

Is Berry's assertion related to the flow of thought here? Aha! The pastoral-agricultural metaphor is a sensory one. The machine metaphor is not, although machines can deliver sensory information unprecedented in the history of our planet. We compare the human body and brain to a machine—the body can be fine tuned, like a car, and the brain is like a computer. The flight from the immediacy of the senses and the gradual attempt to replace this immediacy through technology is perhaps the single most challenging item in the contemporary attempt to refashion learning and to restructure our schools. The subtlety of the challenge is long gone; technology will either serve a valid, balanced sensory base to learning and human development or it will become the ersatz replacement of all that is nonlinear, soft, unpredictable, and natural.

Thinking that the Berry resource could not be outdone in its apparent remoteness to the topic at hand, you find yourself reaching for a book that seems to have been spit out of the shelves. What in heaven's name could Carlos Castaneda's *Journey to Ixtlan: The Lessons of Don Juan* (1972) have to do with the topic? Castaneda describes a piece of his apprenticeship to the sorcerer don Juan in this way: "As a teacher of sorcery, don Juan endeavored to describe the world to me from the very first time we talked. My difficulty in grasping his concepts and methods stemmed from the fact that the units of his description were alien and incompatible with those of my own. His contention was that he was teaching me how to 'see' as opposed to merely 'looking,' and that 'stopping the world' was the first step to 'seeing'" (ix). The question that is raised here is this: Can education play don Juan's role of helping students to see rather than to merely look? Corollary to this question is this: What role does sensory awareness play in this type of education, and where does technology fit into "seeing"?

As if by coincidence your eye catches sight of a stack of back issues of *Chrysalis*. In one issue we find both Berry and Castaneda echoed in lines that trace a relationship among industrialization, market capitalism, and modern patriarchy:

> These elements wrenched the male from his close, seasonally varying contact with land and earth to the machine and the paved urban canyon; from the small, rural community into the huge impersonal city; from work centered in the home and family to work centered in the factory and office; from small-scale, creative craftsmanship into large-scale, automated assembly-line technology; from modest unhurried production for a small, familiar market into highly competitive, success-driven mass production for unlimited profit in a world market. Specialization, mechanization, urbanization brought a great depersonalization of social relations in general of which the alienation of father from son was only one, tragic part (Fleming 1991, 142).

What we have in this passage is the suggestion that the sensory world was dismissed by the ruling patriarchy and, by a not too circuitous logic, the implication that this crushing of the sensory world could easily continue by replacing immediate sensory contact with the orchestrated sensory world of technology. To enhance this thematic caveat about embracing sensory technology we find Doherty's (1993) statement: "With virtual reality, interactive television and 500 channel, fiber optically transmitted high-definition TV already looming on the horizon, the marriage of cinema and computer portends an entertainment experience that does not merely duplicate, reflect or express reality *but promises a superior version of it*" (67; emphasis mine).

What we end up with as we explore the necessary senses in whole-brain education is the fact that the senses may be represented by technology, but technology cannot create a better version of the natural world. The arrogance that flows from the prevailing industrial patriarchal mind would have technology replace the senses just as it replaced the environment with parking lots and pollution.

The fight for sensory whole-brain education is the same fight we have with those who devalue the natural world and still see nature as something to dominate and market for profit. The influx of technology into schools and classrooms is, in itself, a marvelous potential medium for extending the natural world and the senses to deepen the sensory base of learning, but the technology cannot replace the real thing without devaluing the very thing it claims to re-present.

Again your resources present themselves like unexpected gifts, and you uncover an issue of *Chrysalis* that contains Jennifer Logan's (1992) article on the late Rachel Carson, author of *Silent Spring*, the watershed book for environmentalists. In paraphrasing a talk Carson gave in 1951, the author of the article summarizes Carson's perspective by stating, "The belief that humans are inextricably a part of nature lies at the core of her approach to the natural world. To become awe-struck at the beauty of nature is to become conscious of this relationship. It seems to me that if our species is to survive, the capacity to wonder may even be a biological imperative" (68).

Indeed, it is this capacity for wonder triggered by direct immersion in nature that opens neural pathways in the brain, which in turn set the stage for all kinds of associated learning and provide the fundamental blueprint of our own natures to resonate with the world. It is the power of real sensory learning to reveal to us our true natures, our deepest spiritual selves, while simultaneously moving us to grasp at lightning speed an extraordinary knowledge and understanding of life and the world around us.

As if it were listening to the words on this page, a *Yankee Magazine* appeared on my desk. In it was Suki Casanave's (1993) article about a kid's camp in Maine run by the Audubon Society. What proved to be moving about the place is the fact that it is a bare bones camp with nothing other than a camp house, several nature guides, and the wonders of the natural world. The waiting list for the camp's two summer sessions is now up to a year. The concrete experiences kids have with nature is enough. That's it! "Ten days is long enough to crawl through the night woods after a porcupine, to watch an eagle disappear into the distance. Long enough to search out puffins on Eastern Egg Rock. Long enough to creep along with a magnifying glass inches from the ground and follow a trail laid out with a piece of yarn, imagining you are an ant. Long enough to sit alone by the sea and watch dusk descend from an indigo sky. Ten days is long enough to change a life" (68).

While the abstractions of sensory experience produced by technology are important and in many instances powerful adjuncts to direct sensory experience, they engage the brain quite differently. The primary difference is in the fact that the direct interface is not with nature but with the technology itself, which means that the first experience is with technology, not nature. Because of this the eye or the ear or the skin always remains split in attention: part goes toward coping with the media and part toward what is being presented. There is always a subtle stress embedded therein, and this factor alone asks the brain to play a constant role it would not ordinarily play; that is, to monitor various levels of stress both on the external senses as well as the overall stress related to the sensory experience at the level of content.

The greater the technological illusion, the greater the stress, because on an unconscious level one knows that one is really not having the experience one is having. The whole perceptual and conceptual field of experience is not able to let go of this dilemma.

Thus, the technology must eventually be turned off so that the stress level connected with sensory learning from that source may abate, may give way to what it is attempting to replace.

The brain is structured with four lobes (frontal, occipital, parietal, and temporal). For our purposes at this stage of the development of the sensory theme, we focus on three lobes. The parietal lobe, which houses the sensory cortex, is the main player in kinesthetic-tactile experience; the occipital lobe is the key player in visual experience; and the temporal lobe is the key player in auditory experience.

As if to emphasize these three brain domains, an excellent book on learning in the younger years begs for perusal. Filled with tips and activities, Kranyik's *Starting School: How to Help Your Three- to Eight-Year-Old Make the Most of School* (1982) focuses early on "Learning to Discriminate Sights and Sounds," "Large and Small Motor Development," "Play Is Important to Learning," "Learning in an Outdoor Play Area," and "Enjoying the Outdoors." After dealing with music and art activities, the author turns to "Using Television as a Teaching Tool." In essence, Kranyik's book puts the emphasis on these three lobes with activities that are unmediated by technology and involve interaction with both materials and teacher. Dealing with technology follows. We are now at the point where the needs of the three lobes might be reversed and technological "treatment" be the first on the list!

Another way in which the three lobes are important is in motivating children to write. Most teachers supply kids with writing topics so that they subtly lose contact with the rich sensory world they live in as a legitimate source of their writing. Lucy McCormick Calkins (1983) tells us that one teacher, after having witnessed what children brought to school from their own lives, never again assigned a topic to them. "The day Susie and her classmates brought their treasures into school and interviewed each other to learn their stories was perhaps the single most important turning point in the study" (27).

What Calkins points out is that the sensory materials kids gather from their lives are associated with life stories, which kids first share orally through interviews and then make the center-piece of their writings. It would probably not be far off the mark to say that these kids did not bring in TV sets, radios, or even cassette tapes as part of the treasure trove on the day their teacher decided to change the way she assigned writing topics. On the other hand, it would not be surprising if, as the years pass and technology is miniaturized, many of the treasures become wrist TVs, radios, and electronic games. This change is disturbing because it would mean that children are identifying their play, their lives, and their sensory memories with secondhand experience. If this identification be so, it would become even more imperative that teachers take it upon themselves to address brain lobe issues and needs through an even greater emphasis on the unmediated natural world.

A human's sensory system is neither solely innate nor solely learned; it is both. That is why understanding the innate structure of the system as well as what brings that system into full development is critical. To this point our message has been twofold:

1. The major challenge of education is in the competition for the world of the senses, for it is when the senses are fully engaged and challenged that we fully engage and challenge the mind. Medieval philosophy produced the dictum *nihil in intellectu nisi prius in sensu,* or "nothing is in the intellect unless first in the senses."

2. The major competition for the senses is coming from technology, and it is the primary duty of educators today to understand the senses, integrate the senses in a conscious way at all levels of education, and begin a serious integration of technology into the necessary senses of whole-brain learning and teaching.

To address these issues it is important to take a glance at *how the senses evolve,* which we do in chapter 1. Chapter 2 offers sample activities for engaging each of the five basic senses. In chapter 3 we focus on sensory imagination and inner vision, and in chapter 4 we explore artistic sensibility, abstract designs, and reading and writing across the curriculum. In chapter 5 we journey through the use of sound and listening skills, and our focus in chapter 6 is skin, touch, movement, and proprioceptive awareness. Chapter 7 addresses the integration of technology into sensory awareness, and finally, chapter 8 explores the development of spiritual values.

Like the cursor on a computer screen, the high-flying crocodile and peach pit will direct our attention and ground our imagination through each of the chapters. As central images and symbols throughout the exposition, they ask you to think of other symbols and images that might ground what you do as an educator, especially what you do to maintain a vivid, acute, and rich sensory environment as a framework for the teaching and learning that takes place in your classroom. I propose that only by doing so does learning become lifelong.

1

The Evolution of the Senses

The brain constantly needs stimulation to develop, grow, and maintain its organization. It is not really a stable fixed structure . . . In order to keep the organism going in a changing world, the brain has to constantly alter its organization, its circuitry, and even its neuronal structure in response to the changes in experience outside.

—Robert Ornstein and David Sobel

At first, cognition is grounded in the senses. Its second ground is in the imagination. From these two sources of sensory information, abstract reasoning develops. John O. Stevens (1971) states that experience can be divided into three types of awareness:

1. awareness of the outside world—actual sensory contact with objects and events

2. awareness of the inside world—actual sensory contact with inner events

3. awareness of fantasy (5–6)

In each case the mind is embracing some form of sensory information. When teachers develop an awareness of their sensory systems, as well as helping students develop theirs, they feed their mental mills with the experiential grist that makes learning real. To understand how to develop this awareness, we must first look at sensory development both in our species as a whole and in the embryonic development of each individual.

Sensory Development in the Species

Sixty to seventy million years ago a primary function of the early mammalian brain was the analysis of *smells* and *sounds*. This process, necessary for survival at night, is considered the precursor of the functions of the neocortex, and it happens that *the sense of smell is the only sense with a direct route to this higher abstract thinking center.*

The sense of *vision* developed next as mammals increased in size and were hard-pressed to survive during the daytime. This sensory emphasis asks the brain to use visual data to recognize patterns and cues.

Next in line to develop was the sense of *touch,* necessary for climbing, grabbing, and eating. Over time, warm-blooded animals survived, became relatively smaller in size, and developed more complex dendritic branching within their brains as only the fittest lived.

Development of Imagination and Abstract Thought

Somewhere around four million years ago *Australopithecus* developed one-third of the brain-to-body-size ratio necessary for the support of abstract thought and developed a sense of *independence* and the *capacity to hunt.* By somewhere around one million years ago *Homo erectus* exercised a great deal of inner vision, *imagination,* and was capable of *making tools.*

Shortly thereafter *Homo sapien* emerged, the frontal area of the neocortex and forehead moved out, and through the ten billion neurons with more than a hundred trillion connections, *language* developed. *Memory, quick thinking, abstract thought, resourcefulness,* and *ingenuity* became the cognitive qualities necessary for survival in a sensory and often dangerous world. These same qualities are today essential for coping with a world in which the dangers are different but no less sensory.

Since the emergence of *Homo sapien,* the relationship between the sensory world and the evolution of the brain has been an interdependent one. The sensory world changes the brain, which changes the sensory world, which changes the brain, and so on. This drama is reenacted everyday. It should be reenacted daily in a critical and dynamic way in our schools.

In-Utero and Early Childhood Sensory Development

By seven and a half weeks after conception, stimulation around a fetal mouth causes the head to move away from the source of stimulation. By the eighth week the ear begins to form. Between the twelfth and fifteenth weeks *touch* centers around the mouth develop. Other touch reflexes are revealed: stimulation of the palms causes the fingers to close, stimulation of the soles of the feet causes the toes to bend, and stimulation of the eyelids causes the eye muscles to tighten. At this time the fetus grasps, changes facial expressions, sucks the thumb, and swallows.

During the twentieth week *taste* and *smell* develop. Specialized areas of the brain now serve each sense. By the twenty-fourth week, the sense of touch is developed and there are signs that the sense of *hearing* is forming. Between the twenty-sixth and twenty-eighth weeks the optic nerve begins functioning and the sense of *sight* is apparent as the baby responds to light that is shone on the mother's abdomen. In the eighth month and by the thirty-second week, the eyes open and the fetus can see. Dream sleep is prevalent, with 60 to 80 percent of it in REM.

By birth a baby can distinguish colors and shapes within thirteen inches of its face. It responds to various sounds and exhibits a penchant for certain foods and smells. What we see in the sensory development of the fetus is a rough recapitulation of the development of the species as a whole, beginning with a definite emphasis on smell early on and culminating later with the development of vision.

The early development of the sense of smell and taste creates several interesting phenomena. Babies recognize the smell of their own blankets, "allowing the environment to be transported away from home by taking the blanket along" (Gravelle and Rivlin 1984, 76). Within a matter of hours, mothers can usually identify the bassinet of their infant solely by smell.

Fetal hearing through the amniotic fluid is more sensitive than we once thought. "This may help to explain why babies whose fathers-to-be actively speak to them through the mother's belly end up more responsive to their father's voice once they are born" (Rivlin and Gravelle 1984, 78). Newborns exhibit echolocation, a sensory power of hearing we usually ascribe to bats.

Visual development in a newborn is primitive. Relationships that take place within an arm's length of the baby are crucial. Within this focal area the baby develops visual clues about many things. These clues are often intuitive and spatial in nature, calling the right hemisphere into action. When the emotional content is positive, the left hemisphere, usually associated with processing happy experience, registers a happy face or sound.

The visual acuity of an infant at one year is such that the infant is able to identify the gender of another baby even when the baby is dressed in clothes typical of the opposite gender. How can this be? "The answer apparently lies in almost unnoticeable differences in body movement; when an infant is filmed in a dark room with lights attached to its joints so that only the pattern of movement is recorded, other infants can recognize it as a boy or a girl" (Rivlin and Gravelle 1984, 80–81).

Within hours after birth an infant develops tactile sensitivity to pain and pleasure. Built into the feeding process are developmental sensory needs connected with smell, hearing, vision, and touch. The nursing rhythms are regular so that the infant will be caressed and come continuously into contact with the mother. "Our mother's gentle massaging, and the ongoing stimulus of body contact with her, bring these sensory endings to life. Then, with a majority of its sensory system activated, the reticular formation in the old brain goes into full operation. And not to be discounted, all this sensory information is benign, beneficial, and exactly what was expected, what has worked for millions of years" (Pearce 1985, 31).

Rivlin and Gravelle (1984) propose that an infant's sensory system may also be *synesthetic,* which means that sensory systems are so closely connected that such things as seeing a sound or hearing an image are commonplace until the brain becomes specialized, thereby separating each sensory experience into relatively more discrete departments (85–86). What this proposal suggests is that infants are wrapped in a holistic web of sensory overlapping and are being "programmed" with associational memories that influence them for a lifetime, automatically and beneath conscious awareness.

Additionally, this alinear world of infancy manifests itself in the purely subjective manner by which objects are sensed. "Jean Piaget . . . discovered that the perception of the world as consisting of permanent objects whose constancy exists independent of changing viewpoints does not occur until the age of ten to twelve months. For an infant, objects do indeed change their shape and form with movement. Further, until ten to twelve months of age the infant exists in a state of timelessness: Space and time are fused" (Shlain 1991, 138–39). (Of course we learn from Einstein that objects do change shape as well as age when they move!)

Time to Ride the Crocodile Flying the Peach Pit

Somewhere Crocodile, straddling Peach Pit, waits impatiently for you to arrive, to hoist yourself aboard, to sense the silent propulsion as it takes you aloft into the sensory system, a system that was begun eons ago and is reenacted in each miracle of human conception, development, birth, and the days thereafter.

You land at night and watch a small, rodent as it smells the scent of a predator. The rodent stops to listen to anything that might announce the predator's presence, but alas it is too late; the rodent is swiftly devoured beneath a catlike shadow. The Crocodile upon which you sit becomes agitated and tells you that in time the rodent's relatives developed the olfactory and auditory systems to escape the feline creature, which in that moment had outsmarted the rodent.

Peach Pit starts up its quiet flight system and you are aloft once again, flying through time and space to a tree hidden deep in a dank rain forest. You land in the empty nest of an enormous bird.

You watch it fly and circle, beak pointed in zenlike attention at the ground a mile away. "Close your eyes," orders Crocodile. "We can get inside its eyes!" You do. Inside the bird's visual system you feel like part of a telescope reaching into and touching the farthest reaches of outer space, but the lens is facing the other way. Inside the avian lens you see the minutest detail of a chicken-shaped animal, even to the pupils of its eyes. With a sudden turn, the bird descends like a falling rock at a 45-degree angle, and before you can breathe another breath the chicken is grasped tightly in the talons of what appears to be a precursor of an eagle. Out of the corner of its eyes you see feathers float and rock back and forth toward the ground. "Open your eyes," whispers Crocodile. "We have to fly back to the tree and land on the ground beneath it."

Once landed, you hear a screech. Above you, running and jumping from limb to limb, is what appears to be a hairy man. It stops, holding on to a vine with one hand, and in an instant swings into the foliage above and disappears. "Imagine if I could grasp branches like that and move through the jungle as easily! I'd probably be the most feared of beasts. I guess I'll have to settle for my sense of sight and the tactile receptors on my scales and underbelly!" proclaims Crocodile with a smile a mile wide. "Onward, Peach Pit, onward!" he directs his fruit core power source, and you are in flight once again through era after era to the present day.

Crocodile looks you in the eye and by dint of a hypnotic suggestion tells you to close your eyes because Peach Pit is about to take you both inside the world of a human fetus. "It's my kind of environment!" thinks Crocodile. He floats on his back and kicks his feet and laughs when his feet are tickled. Sensors in the fetal mouth and nasal system can taste a little bit of what he tastes of the amniotic fluid in his own mouth and nasal system. The mother's digestive tract movements sound like gently boiling water and he is amazed to watch the fetus react to them. Music and voices from beyond the belly enter the amniotic world. He finds the fetus is calmed by certain of them and irritated by others. What is that glow coming through the abdomen from outside? Croc watches the fetus staring mesmerized at the light source.

Suddenly, the birth canal opens and, contrary to what Croc thought, the process is painless to the fetus. "Heavens! It's a deluge of sensations of light, sound, touch, and odor!" thinks Crocodile. "We are outside. You can open those eyes," he says to you. Peach Pit idles in neutral. "It's all an ocean that delivers a human to the shores of Earthtime and Earthsense," you say to Crocodile. "Yes, maybe if everyone got in touch with their own gestatory period and birth, they'd understand the sensory basis of all learning," responds Croc.

Sensory Awareness in the Sexes

Before we describe the sensory worlds of males and females, we must direct attention to the firm biological basis for asserting that social equality between the sexes cannot be a platform for denying the real differences "hard wired" into the very fabric of males and females. "At a time when efforts are being made to eradicate discrimination between the sexes in the search for social equality and justice, the differences between the sexes are being rediscovered in the social sciences. This discovery occurs when theories formerly considered to be sexually neutral in their scientific objectivity are found instead to reflect a consistent observational and evaluative bias" (Gilligan 1982, 6). The differences are not grounds for social inequities. They are grounds for understanding the complementary qualities that the sexes must share and use in building a society, especially the social phenomenon called school.

Sex-Based Sensory Differences Generalized

In general what can we say about the sensory systems in males and females? The female sensory system is tuned to personal relationships. The female tends to focus on facial expression, tone of voice, touch, and smell as components of personal intimacy and communication. As an infant, her tendency to gurgle more than a male infant is the prologue to her enhanced verbal abilities, necessary for conversation, which is at the heart of interpersonal concerns. Her early play patterns reveal the need for continued reaffirmation of social bonding. In essence, female sensory systems appear to be fundamentally at the service of relationships.

On the other hand, the male sensory system is tuned to action and exploration. His early focus is on things, and even his visual system shows a penchant for discriminating objects in daylight because it is in daylight that movement is easier and more natural. His early play patterns reveal a great deal of movement and physical aggression as well as the need to compete on a physical level. In essence, the male sensory system would appear to be fundamentally at the service of doing something.

An Unfair Reduction and Oversimplification?

Does this description of the sensory differences between males and females do justice to them both? Is this a basis for sexist practices in the schools? "A reform in the method of education can compensate for comparative differences to some extent. It may even give us more women architects or male social workers. But that would involve an acknowledgment of differences which most educationalists have been reluctant to admit, and a degree of positive discrimination which brings with it its own philosophical and political problems" (Jessel and Moir 1989, 66).

Even Gloria Steinem (1992) implies a basic difference in sensibilities in the sexes when she critiques the unfortunate bias toward male tendencies in our culture: "Thus, boys as a group have higher self-esteem because they are literally allowed more of a self and because the qualities they must suppress are less desirable, while girls as a group have lower self-esteem because they are expected to suppress more of themselves and because society denigrates what is left" (257). In effect she is affirming the differences, differences that are easier on boys than on girls because of social values. What she does add, however, is that both boys and girls have to suppress qualities that we assign to the opposite sex. Again, however, society makes the act of suppression more rewarding for males than females because male sensibilities are preferred in the first place.

After observing that the differences between individuals of the same sex are often greater than differences between individuals of opposite sexes, Jane M. Healy (1987) is compelled to conclude that the differences do exist. In essence they boil down to the verbal-spatial and the relational-objectivizing polarities between the sexes.

It is interesting to note that "Dr. E. P. Torrance suggests that sexual stereotypes are a block to creativity, since creativity requires sensitivity—a female trait—as well as autonomy and independence—traits usually associated with males" (Restak 1979, 227). In other words, to be in possession of all of one's creative potential, one must be sensitive to all manner of sensory information, both exterior and interior, as well as the habit of exploring these sensations on one's own. The truly creative person develops both the masculine and feminine traits regardless of gender.

Another interesting piece of research focuses on the leveling off of IQ. Girls tend to level off sooner than boys. In 1971 Muriel Beadle wrote of research done on qualities necessary for continued growth in IQ. The list of qualities is basically masculine in type. Competitiveness, autonomy, self-confidence, bossiness, and the capacity to bounce back from being disciplined ensured that a six-year-old's potential for increasing IQ exceeded the potential of those kids who lacked these traits. Beadle goes on to give an example of this potential, and fortunately the example is of a young girl. "The degree to which a child has these qualities does not come out of the blue on his sixth birthday. If your five-year-old Jennifer, for example, has developed a passion for collecting worms despite your telling her that little ladies don't like worms, should you follow your inclination to flush them down the toilet while she's at kindergarten? Think again: you may be nipping the genius of another Madame Curie" (217).

Would it not seem, then, that the following can be concluded?

1. There are several basic differences in the ways girls and boys perceive and think about what is around and within themselves, and these innate qualities tend to be age related; that is, the innate program of the sexes has more to do with an age-related trigger mechanism than hard and fast permanent differences.

2. It isn't the differences that are the problem but our attitudes toward them.

3. The ideal educational goal is union of the differences, recognition of the differences, nurturing of the differences, and an integration of them.

Unless we meet this goal, we seed our culture with great psychological problems: "If a man or a woman clings to the dominant patriarchal attitude and refuses to make peace with the inner feminine, then she will demand a tribute: When we refuse to integrate a powerful new potentiality from the unconscious, the unconscious will exact a tribute, one way or another. The 'tribute' may take the form of a neurosis, a compulsive mood, hypochondria, obsessions, imaginary illnesses, or a paralyzing depression" (Johnson 1983, 27).

There does seem to be a strong argument for integrating the inner feminine during pregnancy, the neonatal years, and certainly by age six or so when neural structures are becoming relatively organized for life: "In man as in animals, the physical and mental structures can be deeply affected only while the processes of anatomical and physiological organization are actively going on; the biological system becomes increasingly resistant to change after it has completed its organization" (Dubos 1968, 92–93).

Both girls and boys must have their innate needs met and nurtured. They must also be exposed to influences that allow and encourage their innate but possibly less-pronounced opposite-sex sensibilities. The health of individuals and of society depends on it. We may debate the nature/nurture basis for the sexism of sensory awareness, but we cannot pretend that all is given biologically, because we cannot escape the fact that what is given is always being understood subjectively. The great teachers know how to play the chords of nature and to supply alternatives to the acculturation that has limited the number of chords educators have played in the past; we have tended to impose indefensible restrictions on identity.

"The child does not become good or intelligent by having the habits or the opinions of society imposed on him. What he does or knows should be the outcome of a personal reaction on life situations. The truth for me is what I have convinced myself is true: the good I appreciate by the inner light" (Boyd 1967, 172). To be whole-brained, sensory awareness must be whole-sexed. Sex-based differences in sensory awareness cannot be divorced from environmental influences. We make the difference. We give the permissions, create the guidelines, and at some point get out of the way. Homogeneity that violates natural differences as well as violating cultural traditions that are not themselves violations of human dignity is a form of denial. To try to make blacks just like whites in order to redress historical grievances is still racism. To try to make Mexicans just like Americans to redress economic injustice is still imperialism. To try to make males and females fit the same mold to redress violations of human rights is still sexism.

Crocodile's Trip to the Schoolyard

The amphibian watches you impatiently, and you can hear a quiet whirrrr coming from Peach Pit as it gets ready to carry you aboard Crocodile, whose impatient eyes and tapping forefeet signal to you to climb aboard or you will miss the ride. "We're heading for P.S. 20 somewhere in Queens, New York," announces the green swamp dweller. "You can learn a lot by just watching the kids play in the schoolyard," it continues. Your interest is climbing.

Crocodile pulls magic dust from an underpouch and sprinkles it over itself and you. "Got to go for invisibility or we'll scare the kids," Croc says. You grab hold and in seconds the powerful pit has you screaming through the sky with your clothes flapping and your hair blowing.

"There they are!" says an excited Croc. You begin your descent. The first thing you notice is a little boy breaking into the cliques and circles formed by the little girls. In fact he does quite a lot of pushing as he does so.

The boys seem to rule a disproportionate amount of space in the schoolyard to accomplish their play. Only one girl decides to invade male space, shove a boy, and run back, laughing, to her circle.

After landing you walk over to a group of boys. The latest tribal outfit includes open-laced sneakers. A couple of the boys are having flatulation contests. One boy is quite accomplished at armpit farts, but the undisputed champion uses his forearm to produce a sound that one might imagine could come only from the gastrointestinal tract of a dinosaur! Several of the boys are reviewing every conceivable body part as they describe the latest horror movie they watched over pay-per-view cable.

There's the kid with the candy upon whom a cluster of boys fall like vultures. The trading cards come out in another corner of the yard and an argument erupts over the justice of a proposed trade. Meanwhile, a good portion of the yard is devoted to several contests: basketball, touch football, and hockey. One boy is being chased by two girls.

The yard is definitely divided by gender. It seems to you that things haven't really changed since you were a kid. "Seems like old times?" inquires the psychic Croc.

"Let's go over to that group of girls playing jump rope," directs Croc. You notice that in that very controlled space the girls have made the beat of the words and the circling rope into a mesmerizing dance. The tightness of the space in which they organize their play stands out. Everything they do is in close proximity to one another, whereas the boys are much more spread out over the yard.

Uh-oh, one boy has run over and grabbed the rope! Two others pull at the corners of their mouths and make faces and stick out their tongues while making jungle noises. Several of the girls are into the early stages of making up their faces: a little lipstick, a bit of eye shadow, and some blush. All the girls have pocketbooks, but none of the boys do, and only a few have wallets.

Several clusters of girls have cleared spaces, created fantasy houses and rooms, and are using the environment for domestic activities such as tea parties. Some are dancing together. It is only the girls who are walking around in tight groups socializing. Some girls are picking on other kids whom they think are mean, and it is almost exclusively the boys who are picking on other kids for what they consider physical defects, such as being fat. The boys especially pick on one large girl in particular.

Down on one of the ball fields several girls have congregated at the side, practicing cheerleading while the boys play. Now and then they tease the boys. On the swings there appears to be an equal number of boys and girls, although the boys use the swings much more roughly, going side to side and crashing into one another; the girls seem to use the swings just to swing. On the sandpile, the boys, who have almost exclusive use of it, are building tracks, tunnels, and other constructs. There is the exceptional athletic girl who always plays the boys' games, and the exceptional boy who likes to play with the girls, especially when they play house.

Crocodile nudges you. "Look, a teacher is moving out to the jump rope area!" Croc exclaims. You are baffled by the fact that when the teacher is there both boys and girls play together—there is no exclusion except by personal choice; some kids fear embarrassment if they aren't very good at jumping the twirling ropes. You remember Vivian Gussin Paley's (1993) review of Barrie Thorne's book *Girls and Boys in School*. Paley says that for Ms. Thorne, "the relationship between girls and boys is not fixed: teachers can actively enter the equation, even on the playground, to create new patterns of activities with equal opportunities for all" (43). Crocodile looks at you, caught in your own thought.

You return to the spot where you always begin your flight with Croc and Peach Pit. Your imagination has served well as an airport.

Sensory Awareness and Thinking

One of the deepest questions teachers face is how abstract they can get with their students. Or, at what point can sensory material be abandoned in favor of material that requires less of a ground in the five senses? Traditionally, teachers have become more abstract and less sense based as their students have climbed the age/grade ladder in school.

The epistemological conflict evolves this way: Grade school teachers are less embedded in the truth end of the meaning-truth spectrum. They are more content to live with story, experience, and expression, which are really signs of meaning, where life is not black and white. Black/white, either/or truths do have their place; there is a time for rules and drawing definite boundaries. In general, however, in grade school the sensory basis for life and thought and understanding is respected.

In high school there is a tendency for teachers to reverse this emphasis. The truth end of the meaning-truth spectrum dominates, or the pressure to make this reversal is there in the system itself, a pressure that is created by standardized tests, misinformed administrators and school boards, and by a naive interpretation of all sorts of developmental theory.

At the core of the issue are two questions:

1. *Can we trust our senses?*
2. *How do we know what we know?*

Can We Trust Our Senses?

One way of approaching this question is to make a statement we can explore: *Our senses betray us into thinking one thing when the opposite is true.* We have all seen, heard, felt, smelled, and tasted what we thought was one thing but that turned out to be something else. We have been raised to subject sensory awareness to the scrutiny of abstract reasoning and analysis, to the "truthing" process, the either/or judgment of the intellect.

On the other hand, we value sensuality by seeking affection, outdoor life, music, art, food, amusement, dance, laughter and tears, sleep, naps, gatherings, rituals, silence, conversation, games, and intimacy. The sensual itself gives rise to narrative, descriptive, and aesthetic expression, which aims not at truth or falsity but at meaning that is only partly grasped by the razor-sharp cutting edge of intellect. Sensual experience is understood at another level of body and mind. It has an immediacy that gives rise to further nonanalytical expression. It is a world that is never fully understood, a world constantly open-ended, always a world waiting to be explored further. For this reason, a culture dominated by intellect must by its very nature harbor a subtle distrust of the senses and always be marked by a form of alienation from the body.

What, therefore, do we have? On the one hand we have the necessity of the senses, for without them we wither and die. On the other hand we have the intellect, which prevents us from drifting in a sea of sensory data. In a culture that denies the senses, the intellect roams free to create a universe of laws, restrictions, and punishments by which to corral a society. All societies that violate human rights do so primarily by attacking the body. The deepest impressions we have of the Holocaust are the camps where bodies were mutilated, destroyed, and heaped on top of one another. We see this basic image time and again throughout history when a dominant group suppresses the bodies, the art, the writings, the rituals, and the families of those judged by the cold, twisted reasoning of a "superior" race to be disposable. It is not melodramatic to say that this ritual has been reenacted over and over again in our school systems.

Our first connection with the world is a sensory and aesthetic one and our deepest symbolism is conveyed through our art.

Jamake Highwater (1981) puts it this way: "If someone does not experience an aesthetic relationship to what is before him or her, all the information and education will not permit that person to cross the distance that exists between different peoples and, for that matter, between different individuals of the same technological society" (13). In other words, the currency of exchange between people that opens up substantial communication and meaning is a sensory one. Through the immediacy of art (both visual and verbal), we enter one another's real worlds and participate in an intimate way in the symbols that reveal who we are and what makes us tick. Hence, while abstraction and the truth seeking of intellect are important, they must find their place within a primary world of sensation; if they do not, their tendency is to destroy it.

Are the senses trustworthy? Maybe, but that is not the right question. Are the senses the primary world in which intellect is a resident? Yes! "Wherever the world is understood exclusively in terms of discursive facts there can be no access to other worlds" (Highwater 1981, 13). The goal of all good teaching is to make that sensory primary contact with students; only then will students open up to elements that are more abstract. This goal applies across the curriculum. The sensory-aesthetic exchange must come first. The classroom must be a place of feeling, art, poetry, dialogue, and symbol. This exchange can incorporate analytical processes that are at the service of truth without being simultaneously destructive of meaning.

How Do We Know What We Know?

All teachers teach with an implicit philosophy, an implicit response to the question "How do we know what we know?" There is no way around this philosophy. In the modern jargon of teaching styles, we embrace this fact. We recognize that some teachers are more abstract in their style and others are more concrete. Some are more analytical and others are more intuitive. The fundamental polarities have many labels.

However, dare it be said that the most successful of teachers somehow address the sensory basis of all learning? They recognize that, come what may, the only real learning is that which captivates the senses. Even the most abstract content, process, and product require one or more of the five traditional senses in order to be understood. Thus, on a minimal level, successful teachers excite students about what they are doing, challenge them, get the adrenaline moving.

Most students, if they were free to be candid, would say that they have learned almost nothing, even if their grades seem to betray this statement. Why do they feel this way? Because they have not been engaged sensorially in their work. The "head trip" and the memorization and the motivation to get good grades have all conspired to make learning an unauthentic experience. One must feel one's body, one's senses, one's imagination, one's love of the material in the learning process, however abstract the content might be.

Engaging the senses does not mean that learning will be struggle-free; sometimes blood, sweat, and tears must be part of the experience to break through a particularly difficult assignment, which is all part of the immersion in learning that consumes a student and a teacher and takes on a heartbeat all its own. Any attempt to grasp an abstraction is a flesh-and-blood, sensory-based, trial-and-error process in which grades are by-products of the more central concern.

How do we know that we know? We know that we know primarily through our senses. Our evolution individually and corporately is toward abstraction and psychic intuition based on experience. But the experience must be there always.

Additionally, we must participate in a feedback mechanism called "asking questions" in order to fully and authentically enter the experience of finding out how we know what we know. Critical thinking can take place only in an atmosphere of freedom wherein senses, hunches, perceptions, and felt meanings are openly valued. Thinking is a felt experience because it is linked with value, which in turn is linked with sensation (a sense that something feels right or wrong). The best way to prevent students from thinking, or from asking questions, is to devalue the senses.

We know what we know only through expression. All expression requires use of the senses. If we have been cut off from our senses, then what we know will not fully manifest itself. In the rituals of efficiency that schools constantly find themselves pressured into performing (via curriculums that students develop an abstract mastery over), relatively little is valued, for meaning must be felt first and expressed afterwards. Students are made to believe that the results of tests indicate what they know. But this is not how we really know what we know. We come to the point of knowing when we care about something and, from that care, produce something. Whatever that "thing" is will be the truest indicator of what we know as well as whether or not we want to know more, because we care about what we make.

All Aboard the Crocodile Flying the Peach Pit

Landing in the Middle of a Socratic Dialogue

Croc looks at you with one big, dark eye. The other is closed like a safe at Fort Knox. Peach Pit, now snugly lodged in the belly button of old Croc, waits for his stirring. "Let's go, Croc, I've got to settle this issue about thinking and the senses. Let us travel to Greece around the time of Socrates, around 400 B.C.E. It was a time of great discussion about sensation and ideas." Your sense of purpose moves Croc, which in turn moves Peach Pit. In seconds you are aloft and circling Athens, on the lookout for Socrates.

"Land on that hill and wait for me," you suggest to Croc. Croc will have nothing of this. "I'll turn invisible in his eyes. I'll hypnotise him," avers Croc definitively. And so it goes as Croc suggests. The two of you, and Peach Pit traveling as a jewel in Croc's belly, walk alongside the toga-draped Socrates. The conversation starts off politely, with Socrates just a bit annoyed at what seems to be a tic you possess, but it is really Croc nudging you and whispering into your ear when an important point is about to be made.

"And so sensation, according to Democritus, was real because there were these building blocks of the physical called *atoms*. But the whole thing gets less precise when it comes to value. Value doesn't exist as a physical object," says Socrates.

"So, while sensation can be said to be caused by real physical objects outside ourselves, the same cannot be said for what we call value and morality. This is part of the dilemma you are suggesting, Socrates, is it not?" you ask as Croc gives you an approving wink.

"For sure. You see, I believe that reality is not limited to sense perception. You see, sensory awareness exists in space and time because physical objects exist there. However, there is another world that is nonsensory but which has an intimate relation with the sensory. It is the world of ideas," replies Socrates.

"Can we focus on this 'intimate relation' the nonphysical has with the physical?" you inquire. Croc is skipping ahead of you, and dust, which gets in Socrates' eyes, mysteriously rises from the ground every three or four feet. You are amused by Croc's little prank.

"No, not yet. It is important to understand that the mind has a life of its own. An idea can generate another idea without its existing in reality or without its having a referent object you can sense. Mathematics is exactly this. The mind can continually weave one conclusion after another from what you call an equation," states Socrates in a definitive way.

Crocodile is nudging you till it hurts. He whispers into your ear, and for a while it seems as if you are Croc's puppet. "Wait a second, there, Socrates, even the abstract world of mathematics is nothing more than a language of the sensory world, be that sensory world macroscopic or microscopic. The highest abstractions are grounded in the sensory at all times. It's just that we are stretched by these abstractions beyond experience, but they all require proof: sensory, experiential proof," you state emphatically.

"Well, yes, but in the absence of sensory proof, the mind is still free to wander," Socrates replies.

"In our day, a man by the name of Einstein is considered to have been one of the greatest scientists of all time. And he said that imagination was the most important gift we have. It was by use of his imagination that he discovered what we call the theory of relativity. Imagination is an inner sensory world that produces pictures, feelings, and sensations of all types, and it allows us to actually see into the future," you suggest.

"You raise the central issue here. It is the issue of what is real. In my time we argued about change and permanence. It seems that sense perception is always changing; things are never the same. On the other hand, there does seem to be permanence. The sun, which is a central symbol for us when we talk about reality, is always changing yet always not changing. It changes because it comes and goes; it remains the same because it is always coming and going," replies Socrates.

Croc whispers into your ear that you better get to the point, 'cause you have to return to the airport of your imagination. Peach Pit needs a rest.

"I read Plato's 'Allegory of the Cave' and I am led to believe that in the final analysis Plato meant to state that we are born with an inner light that can help us see the inner truth or reality of things, that education has as its highest goal directing each soul to its own light and from that light to understand life," you proclaim almost sermonically.

"Quite true. This inner form is active and creative. You see, Plato did not mean to deny the sensory world, but he did mean to deny that we are passive recipients of sensation, or what you might call clay that such sensation manipulates. What I am trying to say is this: Our lives are sensory, but the sensory is not merely a materialistic impression upon our bodies and our imaginations. We are living clay and as such we also form and give shape to what shapes us. In other words, when you return to your teachers in the world you come from, remind them that they must do two things if they are to be great teachers. First, they must engage all the outer and inner senses of their students. Second, and here is the crux of our dialogue, they must engage and elicit from them their own inner light, which will not only illuminate their experience but also prepare them to derive and shape ethical sense out of the world," concludes Socrates.

"Of course. Now I know why I stopped to talk with you. Teachers must understand that sensory awareness involves an innate knowledge that we are born with, a knowledge that illuminates our experience, gives meaning to it, and helps us discover what we hold in common about life as well as what is peculiarly individual about sensation as far as we are concerned. Thank you so much for helping to clarify that sensory awareness is not merely materialistic but holistic, that sensation and the mind are partners. We use the term *sensory* because sensory awareness is founded in sensation of some sort. We say *awareness* because it is also equally founded in innate qualities of the mind," you summarize proudly.

Peach Pit, hidden securely in Croc's belly, begins the whirring sound that signals it is time to go. As Socrates returns to full consciousness he hears a voice in the sky but doesn't look up. Flying was uncommon 2500 years ago.

2

Sample
Activities for
the Senses

Now there is nothing in the understanding, which was not before in the sense. And therefore to exercise the senses well about the right perceiving the difference of things, will be to lay the grounds for all wisdom, and all wise discourse, and all discreet actions in one's course of life. Which, because it is commonly neglected in schools, and the things which are to be learned are offered to scholars, without being understood or being rightly presented to the senses, it cometh to pass, that the work of teaching and learning goeth heavily onward, and affordeth little benefit.

—John Amos Comenius

The activities in this chapter may be used at any level if you adapt them in such a way as to be respectful of the age and experience of your students.

The Kinesthetic, Touch, and Motion: Playing the Parietal Lobe

Goal of the Activity

This activity should lead to verbal and visual expression. The content or the heart of the activity involves becoming more familiar with oneself and some aspect of the natural world. The activity should lead to written or artistic expression about oneself and the natural world.

Phase A: Jump Rope

Have students do this activity in groups of four: two to hold the rope and two to do the jumping. The pairs switch roles after five minutes. While jumping rope the jumpers call out names of things from nature (animals, plants, insects, oceans, mountains, fish, and so on) using each letter of the alphabet in turn (aardvark, bear, coyote, deer, eel, frog, germs, himalayas, iceberg, and so on). After each pair has had five minutes to call out these names, the theme switches to self. While jumping rope the jumpers say how they are like at least five of the names they called out ("I am like a coyote because I love the moon at night"). Each pair has five minutes. When finished, each group shares what they did. After the sharing, each student takes five minutes to record some notes about the event. The notes can be reflective.

Phase B: Earth, Air, Fire, Water

This activity requires a bowl of dry earth and a bowl of moist earth, air around us, matches and kindling, and bowls of hot and cold water. The students work in *new groups* of four. As in phase A, two students generate the mechanics while two go through the activity. After five minutes the roles change.

Two of the four are blindfolded. Bowls of dry earth and moist earth are placed before them. The blindfolded students place one hand in the dry earth and the other hand simultaneously in the wet earth. The blindfolded students spend a minute quietly touching and sifting through the earth samples. Without cleaning their hands, each then places one hand in hot water and the other in cold water, engaging in the same concentrated sensing of the water as they did the earth. When a minute is up, the students remove their hands from the water and let them air-dry. Have students be aware of the naturally drying action of the air.

The next two steps are ideally done outdoors; you can make adjustments to accomplish the fundamentals of the activity indoors. Blindfolded students from each group are led around until they find the spot where the air smells freshest to them. At their personal fresh air spots, the students quietly breathe deeply in a concentrated way, trying to notice the effects of the scents on and in their bodies and minds. The last step of this phase requires the students to light kindling in a safe area and listen to it burn, smell the burning embers, and safely hold their hands over the fire to sense the heat and feel the smoke and warmed air glide over their skin.

When the sensory part of the activity is over, the groups meet and compare notes, focusing especially on which of the activities in this phase had the most and least impact on each individual. They select a spokesperson for the group. The spokespeople report to the large group about responses in each subgroup. After this sharing, each student spends at least five minutes recording notes about the event.

Phase C: Mirroring

This event requires students to work in pairs in front of the large group in approximately four-minute segments. After choosing partners, the class gathers in a circle. The first pair walks to the center of the circle. For the first minute they stand one behind the other. The one in the rear mirrors the movements of the one in front, then they change roles. For the second two minutes they face each other and do the same thing, with one exception; they may look only into each other's face.

It is not necessary for every pair to do this on one day. The whole and parts of this activity for the parietal lobe can be stretched out over time. You might stop the action after three or four pairs do the mirroring, then have each of the pairs share anything they felt during the activity. When they are finished, have the rest of the class comment and ask questions of the pairs. Conclude the event with five minutes of note recording.

Before moving on to Phase D, review what we have done thus far: We have tapped the kinesthetic sense by jumping, handling, and mimetically acting something out. We have also associated these body movements with thinking, speaking, discussing, and writing. In essence we have grounded anything that is abstract about thinking, speaking, and writing in a physical, sensory experience.

Phase D: The Abstraction

Now help students draw as much as they can out of these experiences. Will they do it through writing? Will they do it through art? Will they do it by adding on some reading and research? How do their activities connect to anything in the curriculum? Is it relevant to any curricular discipline?

It is best to approach these experiences in an interdisciplinary manner, but if one must divide the disciplines the following are possibilities.

> **Language Arts:** You have the basis for poems, essays, research projects, and speeches. Poetry, for example, can be based on self, jumping, the four elements, and the essence of a mirror (the fantasy of becoming a mirror). It is always interesting for the teacher as well as the student to confer about what the student plans to do or has begun. Get into the feelings, images, and ideas that are percolating. Students who draw a blank or are indecisive may need direction. Sometimes the direction you give a student stimulates something quite different from what you expected and the student makes her own decision.
>
> **Social Science:** Students can study, compare, and report on the role movement plays in various cultures. You might want to limit the comparisons to dance and ritual. The reports should be verbal, visual, and kinesthetic (the kids do the dances and demonstrate the rituals).
>
> **Science:** Isn't this an ideal opportunity to study the muscles and the joints in order to understand what is physically involved in the specific movements the students have used? Additionally, isn't this an ideal time to study a bit of nutrition (for example, what nourishes these muscles and

what does not)? Each student or team can study a specific muscle area exercised during phases A through C. A creative way of making a presentation would be to interview the muscles and the bones in joint areas.

"Educational Kinesiology" addresses utilizing movement to increase learning while decreasing stress, which inhibits learning. This idea underscores the importance of the physical and sensory as fundamental components of the learning process across the curriculum. The founders of Educational Kinesiology, Paul and Gail Dennison, created "Edu-K" and "BrainGym," which aim to balance brain functioning to increase and maximize learning, specifically in the areas of reading, spelling, and math.*

Vision: Playing the Occipital Lobe

Goal of the Activity

Peter Russell (1979) states, "Visual images are generally much better remembered than words. So much so that visual recognition is practically perfect" (114). There is no one who does not learn through visual input and internal imagery. Anees A. Sheikh and Katherina S. Sheikh (1985), founders of the American Imagery Institute, call for the use of imagery as a "legitimate and valuable human function in the educational process" (10). The following activities have as their function to provide and stimulate visual information that will, in turn, elicit higher-order thinking that will result in work that combines the visual and the verbal.

Utilizing External Images

For whatever it is worth and however one analyzes the relationship between seeing and doing, by the time the average child reaches eighteen he has witnessed eighteen thousand simulated murders on TV (Cannon 1993, 19). And, depending on the socioeconomic setting as well as the solidarity within the family, the average American child has witnessed real-life violence. A great number

---

*Contact: Educational Kinesiology Foundation, P.O. Box 3396, Ventura, California 93006-3396. You can order *Education in Motion: A Practical Guide to Whole Brain–Body Integration for Everyone* from Zephyr Press, P.O. Box 66006, Tucson, AZ 85728-6006.

of images that children digest from the external environment have been violent ones. One of the roles art and visualization play in education is to counterbalance these experiences and in so doing to play the depths and riches of the occipital lobe, visual memory, and visual thinking. Visual thinking is at the heart of metaphor, which itself is at the core of higher-order thinking skills. There is a beauty and a counterbalancing peace in imagery work that unlocks for kids experiences that help to offset, explain, and place in a wider context the catalogue of disturbing and distorting images they keep within themselves.

The Mandala Exercise

A mandala is "a circular design containing concentric geometric forms, images of deities, and symbolizing the universe, totality, or wholeness in Hinduism and Buddhism" (*Webster's New World Dictionary*, 2d ed., s.v. "mandala"). Mandalas are also used in contexts outside the religious framework in which they developed. Carl Jung (1973) used mandalas in therapeutic work with his patients. More recently, the idea of using mandalas to elicit ideas, promote writing, and stimulate discussion has been popping up in books for teachers. (Galyean 1983; Murdock 1987; Williams 1983).

Step 1: If possible, copy the mandala that appears on page 39. Cover the title, "Mandala of Peace," so that your students do not know the intent of the artist-student. Direct discussion and writing with the question "What do you think the artist was trying to communicate through this mandala?" When all that can be shared has been discussed, reveal to the students the title of the mandala.

Step 2: Hand out blank circles with a core and three concentric circles within (copy the circle on page 40). Have students draw two lines through the circle to make four equal quadrants. Explain to them that when they start their first mandalas they should keep the mandalas balanced by repeating the items they draw in one quadrant in one of the other quadrants. They will catch on.

Step 3: After absorbing the format of mandala design and balance, students should create their own mandalas. When they are finished, have them assign a theme to the mandala

as Kelly Dubois, a tenth-grade student, did with "Mandala of Peace."

Step 4: In this final step, students explain their mandalas in writing and orally before the class. It might be interesting to exhibit the mandalas first, have the kids assign a theme to each, then compare their impressions to the artists' explanation.

Follow-up: An activity that one class enjoyed was painting a large mandala on the wall of the classroom based on a theme (their issue was "searching for self"). Students then described the various sections of the mandala, and told what each part represented.

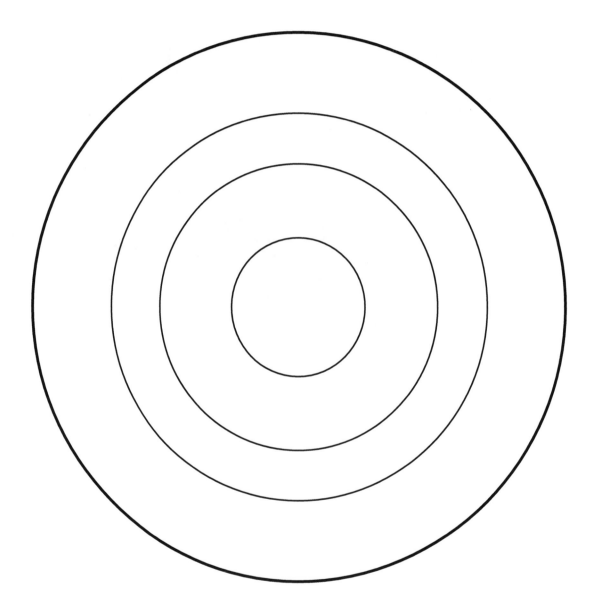

Sound and Sense: Playing the Temporal Lobe

Goal of the Activity

Michael Murphy (1992) tells us that some orchestra leaders can tell if a single violin is playing the wrong notes during a concert, even while a hundred or more instruments are simultaneously making their contributions to a piece (66). Of course this skill represents an extraordinary development of a particular sense, but it also points out to us how really sensitive our ears are. For most of us this sensitivity is beneath conscious awareness; however, what we hear beneath this awareness affects us.

In reflecting on his own relationship with sound, Don Campbell says of his early years, "Music was the world. Everything was vibration, feeling, and movement. Although I could hardly name it with words, I felt the sacred presence of life through sound . . . Silence was impossible. Quiet was possible from the outer world, so all the internal inventions of sound could be heard. Trees, cars, and even clouds had their rhythms. Words I did not understand had melodies. The world was SOUND" (Brewer and Campbell 1991, 13). Using sound and music has become a basic skill for teachers, for sound and music are fundamental to life. To overlook this fundamental principle in teaching is a breach of contract with children whose capacity to learn is connected to sound, the sound of many voices, especially the sound of their own authentic voice.

The following activity is intended to relax students so that they might hear the sound of their inner voice and bring it into the open through music, sculpture, drawing, writing, and discussion.

The Focused Listening Exercise

Step 1: Gather the following materials together: a fork, a spoon, a pie plate, a balloon, a harmonica, a sheet, sandpaper, a small block of wood, tissue, a large bowl of water, matches, and a soundtrack of Gregorian chant. Place all these objects in a line in the center of a circle of students.

Step 2: Have students lie down with their heads pointed toward the center of the circle. By each student's head place a piece of paper, a pencil, and seven crayons in basic colors.

Explain to them that they may either close their eyes or keep them open, but what is most important is that they really concentrate with their ears. Tell them you are going to turn on a sound called Gregorian chant and that there is scientific and experimental evidence to show that the sound energizes the brain (Weeks 1991, 48). Ask them to let the sound relax them.

Step 3:   When students have relaxed into listening, ask one student at a time to rise and select one of the objects that you placed in the center of the circle. Have the student create a sound with the object while the other students simply listen. Repeat this process until each student has had a chance to create a sound.

Step 4:   Now ask students to sit in a circle with their heads pointing away from the objects while you carefully experiment by creating sounds with the objects. The most important aspect of the activity is the concentrated listening.

Step 5:   Group the students in fours. Have the quartets select objects from the center of the circle to create some kind of "band sound." Other students can either continue facing away from the center or face the center with eyes closed. When all the quartets have played, it is time to write, draw, and paint.

Step 6:   Before moving on to this next step, take a break, preferably one that allows for movement. Regather the kids and ask them to sit comfortably where they can easily hear you make sounds with the objects. They should have with them paper and pencil. With the Gregorian chant playing almost inaudibly in the background, begin to play with each object. The students should write about each object and the sounds they hear. Ask students to see if they can compare each sound to a sound they have heard something else make. Ask them to describe the sound they like best and the sound they like least.

Step 7:   With paints, paper, colored pencils, and magic markers available, play the Gregorian chant at an acceptable audible level. Ask students to use the materials to create the feeling they have while listening to the music. The artwork should not be of real objects but simply an expression in form and color of what the sound does to them, what feeling it inspires in them. When they are finished, ask them to give their art titles. Display the art.

Three Interdisciplinary Extensions of the Activity

In *language arts* students research the use and meaning of sound in a variety of cultures and produce a paper explaining cultural sound. At the same time they can prepare presentations that require them to dress up in that culture's costume or fashion, cook and distribute food representative of the culture, and create a museum of artifacts made by its people. This aspect of the project falls under *social studies,* and the project can be brought full circle by a *scientific* focus on technological progress in the culture.

Nosing Around

Goal of the Activity

Utilizing the sense of smell within academic disciplines may seem far-fetched. Yet, if the senses are intimately connected to perception and concept formation, we cannot overlook any of them. Because the sense of smell is associated with such basic functions (sexuality, eating, digestion, death, and life), through it we enter a realm of immediacy that is very delicate, very primal, and easily dismissed on a conscious level. Yet our lives are permeated by near obsessions with odor. Is there not a perfume by this very name, Obsession? Does not the smell of certain foods drive us wild? What about flowers, freshly mown grass, sea air? What about those pheromones that are precursors to sexual arousal? There is even a smell associated with holiness called "the odor of sanctity."

It is a challenge to use this sense to enhance basic skills in writing and art. The following activity is intended to help students and teachers develop links between smell and ordinary academic disciplines.

The Focused Olfactory Exercise

Step 1: Gather the following materials: several types of essential oils (or you could use perfumes and colognes), a live flower in a vase of water, a handful of rich earth, a bar of unscented soap, a jar of peanuts, and an old sneaker. Place them on a table a foot or so from one another.

Step 2: Ask students to slowly take in the aroma of each object, and as soon as they return to their seats, to make notes on their response to each odor. Repeat the exercise with students blindfolded, again having them take notes. Tell students that they are now going to make associations with the aromas. Here are some possible associations they may make:

1. Which smells oldest and why?

2. Which smells youngest and why?

3. What emotions can you identify with each smell?

4. Is there another natural object that smells like each of the smells?

5. Can you associate a location (house, beach, store) with each of the smells?

6. Do any of the smells connect with school or anything else associated with school (building, books, particular classrooms, labs, lockers)?

7. Where would you (each student) find each smell? Make a list.

The next step in the exercise is to *personify the smells* in one of two ways:

1. If each smell were a person, would each smell be a friend of yours? Students should explain why.

2. The scene is a card game and all the smells show up to play. Before they play, they have a conversation about what they did that day.

For additional practice of writing skills, after students have completed these activities you might have them write a traditional five-paragraph essay about the three smells they liked most.

An artistic response to the aroma exercise might be to create a still-life portrait of an object on the table and, if possible, to include the smell on the paper that contains the portrait.

Tasting Life

Anne Moir and David Jessel (1991) claim that women are more sensitive to bitter tastes and men more sensitive to salty tastes. Robert Ornstein and David Sobel (1987) suggest that during our evolutionary past our sweet tooth was responsible for helping us avoid poisonous plants (sweet things are rarely poisonous) as well as for the development of small muscle movement via the gathering of edible delectibles (62).

Our schools feed children every day and many have home economics programs that fill hallways with various aromas from recipes. Candy is a major fund-raising item, and between classrooms, rectangular soda machines light up the short and long hallways and focus the eye on the refreshment of choice.

Yet in spite of the pervasive presence of the gastronomic universe, the sense of taste is another of the senses that we seem to do little with across the curriculum. One teacher recently celebrated the food that appeared in *Cold Sassy Tree* by recruiting other teachers and her students to prepare culinary delights from the book. This type of activity could easily become a generic use of the gustatory realm to enhance literature and to celebrate the setting and ambience of a story.

Goal of the Activity

The following attempt to involve and address the sense of taste in a broad curricular fashion has as its primary purpose the demonstration that our senses are our most immediate source of experience. From them, we can derive the written word, feel a piece of art begin to take shape in our mind and in our feeling body, and provide content for research and the development of new recipes and uses for food itself.

The Focused Taste Exercise

Gather the following items: a cup of sugar; a half a cup of salt; several vegetables tomatoes, lettuce, and celery; a bit of mustard, some olive oil, and potato chips.

Give each student a paper plate, a plastic fork, and a spoon. Place samples of all tasteables on each student's paper plate.

While they taste, students should hold their noses. Have students sample the olive oil first. At this point, they are tasting for texture. Students should concentrate on the texture of the olive oil and slowly let go of the nose to sense the shift in the sensory experience once smell is let into the process. Students should record this first taste experience, mentioning any feelings and associations the taste has for them. Continue the process with the remaining samples, again having students jot down notes after each taste.

Next have students give symbolic value to each item. For example, one might equate olive oil with inspiration because it is slippery, slippery is what one has to be to get away with certain things in life, and to get away with certain things one must be suddenly inspired with the proper action. When students have attached values to each taste, you might have them try creating a story in which the main character tastes the items that give her those qualities.

This step might be followed by a metaphor game in which you list each item alongside a list of unconnected items. Equate each tasteable with as many items as possible in the other list, being sure to explain the connection:

Taste Items	Other Items
sugar	lightning
salt	an owl
lettuce	a thumb tack
tomatoes	a girdle
celery	a sneaker
mustard	a checker
olive oil	a dollar bill
potato chips	a mosquito

Here's an example of equating a tasteable item with an item from the other list and explaining the connection: The **mustard** hit my tongue like **lightning** and sent a charge through my mouth that brought tears to my eyes. Its sharp taste zapped my tongue, which lay in the groove of my mouth like bark from a tree caught in a thunderstorm.

We know that the sense of taste develops early in utero. It is crucial because its role in the act of eating means that it is also an important player in the creation of community. Food is used not just to fill a physical craving for nourishment, but also to bring people together in community to share, laugh, cry, celebrate, and grieve. It ought not be denied in academic circles as a valid base from which to write, create art, and celebrate curricular achievement.

What Is Crocodile Doing while Peach Pit Is Getting a Tune-Up?

Crocodile is peering at a small snake sunning itself on a rock half-exposed from the water. Moving cautiously through the water, with eyes visible like two floating marbles, Croc edges ever so much closer to the snake. His mouth begins to water in the water. Just as he is about to rise and snap at the snake, it disappears, and in its place appears an enormous sundae dripping with hot fudge sauce, nuts, and whipped cream. Wonderful! When Croc moves gently to devour this delight it, too, disappears, and in its place a steaming plate of spaghetti and meatballs with hot garlic bread appears. Croc is going mad. His favorite pasta! This time he moves even more cautiously toward the rock, and when he snaps as gently as any crocodile could be asked to do when eating, presto, the spaghetti disappears. In its place a large hand appears with a sign that reads "Expert Under-the-Chin Crocodile Scratcher."

This is brutal. Croc loves to have his underside scratched, especially under his lower jaw. He can feel the pleasure as he sidles up to the hand, which scratches under Croc's chin once and disappears, leaving Croc in a trance. A beautiful heron stands on the rock playing a sweet violin that moves Croc deeper into his trance, where he dreams of the color green and sees himself as king of green. He remains in his dream until awakened by Peach Pit, whose engines are now in top form, ready to continue Croc's adventure into the senses.

3

Sensory Imagination and Inner Vision

Genius is childhood recaptured.

—Baudelaire

Early Appearances

If you were asked what characteristics seem to be the province of childhood, you might say imagination, receptivity, and impressionableness.

Dreaming, fantasy, make-believe, and imagination coupled with an incredible sensory receptivity seem to be the constant companions of childhood. Becoming an adult often means growing out of these frameworks of knowing, relating, and being. Yet the happiest and most alive adults I know are the very ones in whom these traits are most evident. I think it has become safe to say that instead of adulthood being identified with the denial of these cornerstones of the soul, maturity is an evocation of the growth, development, and understanding of these mental and somatic powers. Indeed, education must recognize these modes of perception and encourage their development by consciously using them.

Quite a bit of work has been done to understand the phenomenon of *imaginary friends* in childhood. They provide companionship and allow children to experiment with language and various roles. Often the imaginary friend is a listener who understands the fears and anxieties of the child. Generally, these friends are regarded as a healthy and necessary step in the cognitive development of children. If you happen upon your preschooler conversing with such a friend, it is something to cherish. Yet we think that a sign of maturity is finally giving up the imaginary friend. If a child continues to have such a friend, chances are that *psychosis* will come to mind. To inadvertently stumble upon an adult speaking to an imaginary friend would certainly disturb us. Yet this attitude may be changing.

Adults sublimate their fantasies in reading or writing fiction, in theater, in rehearsing a speech or something they might want to say to a real person. Thus we end up dichotomizing development. If it is fine to have imaginary friends up to a certain age, after which they must be given up and replaced with real friends, then where does this cognitive skill based in the imagination go? This either/or separation of one reality from another seems to belong to an outmoded concept of what consciousness is all about and what the orthodox role of imagination is supposed to be at a particular age.

Pretending to be someone else is another dimension of childhood imagination that we call *acting* when adults do it. In fact there is evidence that children who pretend to be someone else often uncover hidden talents. Impulsive children who pretend they are someone else equal the performance of other children on the Matching Familiar Figures (MFF) test; impulsive children who do not pretend do not (Chance 1987, 20).

In his classic work *The Origins of Consciousness in the Breakdown of the Bicameral Mind,* Julian Jaynes writes of the duality of the brain, which, he claims, at one time was weighted toward the right hemisphere or what he interprets as a time of preconscious mind. Through the right hemisphere were heard the voices of gods and revelations, driving individual and tribal behavior. Poetry, song, belief, and worship were the workings of the right hemisphere and still remain strong influences on behavior, but they are considered to be not quite what is defined as the conscious mind.

There is an assumption in his work that consciousness is a pure state of structural operation that can exist only divorced from and uninfluenced by the right hemisphere, and that human evolution shows the gradual decline and breakdown of this bicamerality. It's a wonderful book, but like the works of Descartes, it relies upon the very thing it hopes to prove is on the way out, that is, imagination. Andrew Greeley (1993) tells us that social researchers must use their creative imaginations to deal with whatever information they have in order to construct a hypothesis, that they are not uninfluenced by hunches, expectations, and personal knowledge (70–75). We are as much what we imagine as we are the logic by which we assume we control the world, and probably more so.

What would you think if it were suggested that imaginary friends were real and that the sensory world of childhood was more receptive to a variety of influences than that of adulthood? In applying Ken Wilber's (1980) model of consciousness (prepersonal, sub-personal, personal, supra-personal, trans-personal), Thomas Armstrong (1985) suggests that childhood imagination spins out monsters, fairies, nature spirits, ghosts, poltergeists, spiritual beings, light forms, and entities as children pass in and out of these various stages. In some cases there may be evidence that the beings are not fictitious but that the child's receptivity is so open that things with which adults are denied contact appear to her.

In general there is overwhelming evidence that children possess imaginations that are powerful and that parents and teachers often don't understand or know how to deal with, much less capitalize on, to help them develop. There is a lot of evidence showing there is a gradual repression of imagination by anyone in charge of the maturation process of children. Most adults walk around in a state of unrecognized grief over the abandonment of imagination in their lives. In its place they are often nurtured by cynics and skeptics whose razor-sharp analysis excises the most powerful force in human development without which life dries up.

We can use these two imaginary tendencies of children as the basis for classroom activities throughout the curriculum, K through 12. By using them we are tapping deep energies that will seem eventually very familiar to the students because they will prod vague memories of a time when imaginary friends and pretending to be someone else were the turf of childhood.

Imaginary Friends Exercise

A. The basic activity is simply drawing the friend, describing the friend, and presenting the friend to the class. It would also be helpful for the class to ask the presenter as many questions as they can about the imaginary friend. Versions of this exercise can be done at any level. Of course this basic beginning can evolve into more in-depth art, creative writing, research on friendship, song writing, and video production.

B. This activity asks the student to create a dialogue with an imaginary friend and, if possible, to act it out. The dialogue ought to end with the suggestion that they both go on a trip. This suggestion leads to the student planning a trip across the United States for the two of them. Involved in this planning are using map skills, taking care of a vehicle, finding places to stay, making lists of things to do, and figuring out the finances needed. After the imaginary trip, the student pretends to be the imaginary friend, gives a presentation of the trip to the class as the friend, and answers questions.

C. With an imaginary phone the student calls an imaginary friend who lives in another time. This activity provides an opportunity for the student to focus on history, geography, science, art, and other areas, as the imaginary friend could be someone related to a famous person or could actually be the famous person. This exercise could take many twists and turns, such as the imaginary friend consulting with another imaginary friend who helps answer any questions that may come up in the initial phone call.

D. Set up imaginary pen pals. Pairs of students pretend to be famous people. In this way students personalize the learning of history, literature, and any of the other disciplines. In effect you get two students pretending to be someone else and finding in each other an imaginary friend.

Pretending to Be Someone Else Exercise

A. The student writes a scenario in which a fictitious character emerges; for example, a flying saucer lands from another galaxy and a friendly alien steps out. For two or three weeks the student then maintains a diary as if he were the alien.

B. The student creates a totally fictitious persona by doing the following:

1. making a birth certificate

2. writing a birth announcement that would appear in a newspaper

3. creating a family album (either draw or create a photo album from old photos or new ones of people who pose and possibly dress up in period costumes)

4. making up the contents of a wallet

5. arranging paraphernalia that are prized by that person

6. developing "copies" of letters that person has written to friends and loved ones

7. creating an outfit worn by that person at a particular time in her life

8. dressing in the outfit and arranging an exhibition of all the above items and inviting students, teachers, parents, and friends to come to the exhibition

C. This exercise is intentionally multicultural in that it asks that the student pretend to be a person from another race, religion, and socioeconomic background. Here are some possibilities:

1. Become Martin Luther King Jr.'s daughter during the last ten days of his life.

2. Become John Paul Getty's son, being sure to deal with the fact that his inheritance is billions of dollars.

3. Become Emiliano Zapata defending the peasant class of Mexico and its call for land reform.

4. Become a witch condemned at the Salem witch trials.

5. Become Jackie Robinson during the early years when he became the first black man to break into the all-white bastion of professional baseball.

6. Become Babe Dietrickson Zaharis, one of the first women to challenge men in golf, baseball, and track and field.

7. Become a member of a Japanese family who was placed in an American internment camp during World War II.

8. Become any great American Indian tribal leader who stood up to the cavalry as it attempted to move the Indians off their lands.

9. Become the brother or sister of someone who has died of AIDS and who is remembered in the AIDS quilt.

10. Become Anne Frank as she hid from the Nazis.

> **Note**: In pretending to be any of these people, students can brainstorm a list of things they plan to do as their assumed identities and sign a contract to do so. When the contract is fulfilled they then present it to the class. Videotaping the presentations and making them available during parent conferences is a potent way to display what a child is capable of, and it makes the conference more practical in nature.

Dreams and Daydreams

Carl Jung (1965) tells us that he had a dream, the first he could recall, between the ages of three and four. This dream, Jung tells us, was "to preoccupy me all my life" (11). The dream of an underground phallus would eventually, at around the age of fifty, become clearer in meaning to him, but what continued to amaze him was the appearance of the specific dream imagery at such an early age, imagery that he could not completely connect with personal experience.

There is a marvelous book that one sometimes hears of when there is a need to communicate something about perception, habit, limitation, and thought. In Edwin Abbott's *Flatland* (1983) only two-dimensional reality exists. When, after being told of the third dimension by a sphere, the narrator breaks through into three dimensions, he attempts to convince others in his world of this three-dimensional world. At first he tries to persuade his family, but to no avail. He attempts to deal with it euphemistically so as not to arouse too much contempt. Finally, he decides to throw caution to the wind at a large meeting at Flatland's Assembly Hall. He says, "At first, indeed, I pretended that I was describing the imaginary experiences of a fictitious person; but my enthusiasm soon forced me to throw off all disguise, and finally, in a fervent peroration, I exhorted all my hearers to divest themselves of prejudice and to become believers in the Third Dimension" (117). He is arrested and sent to prison, where he writes his memoirs, hoping that they "may find their way to the minds of humanity in Some Dimension, and may stir up a race of rebels who shall refuse to be confined to limited Dimensionality" (119).

Dreams and waking thought can be likened to the different dimensions that seem to have no relationship to one another. In the context of school experience dreams represent Flatland's third dimension. It is almost heresy to suggest that "Flatschool" ought to pay homage to the "dream dimension." Yet how can such an important experience be avoided so persistently in a student's curricular experience? Why do we avoid dream sharing, dream journaling, dream writing, and dream dramatics in our curriculum? Is it because, in part, we associate these activities with psychotherapy? If this were the case, we would have to quit teaching, for our very language itself, used as it is in psychotherapy, would have to be abandoned. Perhaps it is closer to the truth that we are simply not in the habit of dealing with our dreams—just as many are not in the habit of playing baseball. There is a lot of baseball literature and there are many movies to accompany it, but one would shy away from teaching it if one were not accustomed to its vocabulary, lore, and overall value in our culture. When we look at it this way, incorporating dreams into the curriculum is simply a matter of making dreamlife a focus of one's waking thought and from that concentration gradually developing curricula that tap dream experience.

Daydreaming is often interpreted by teachers as inattentiveness. Displayed by people of all ages, it is intensified at certain developmental stages and at other nondevelopmentally related periods, such as when we are tired. Its content may not be as symbolic as that of ordinary sleep dreaming, but it may be as important. Students who sit near windows sometimes stare off into the sky or at trees; sometimes they are flooded with visual memories or fantasies. Sometimes students appear to be the epitome of attentiveness but are really off into the wild blue yonder. It is the artful teacher who knows when to invade the daydream and when not to. Daydreaming is a time of brain growth when the contents of thought are not controlled by rationality. It is a time when the brain feeds on free associating, a randomness that it needs to remain healthy and sane. As with regular dream experience, the question is, What can be done with it inside the curriculum?

Dream Exercises

A. A good beginning might be to purchase the *Jungian-Senoi Dreamwork Manual* and become familiar with one of the best overviews of dreamlife, remembering dreams, journal keeping, and exercises such as dialoguing with one's dreams (Williams 1980). One of the best things to do is to begin keeping a journal on the people, places, things, and events in your own dreams. From this experience, extrapolate a method of teaching children and teens to do the same. Encourage as much nonjudgmental description as possible. Have them keep a journal of all their dreams and a separate one with examples that they feel comfortable sharing with classmates. Combine art and writing and set up a dream museum of each child's best work. Have students peruse the gallery, and follow the perusal with a discussion of the dreams they found most interesting. In no way should the discussion become analytical or interpretive. Questions should simply attempt to get an accurate description of the dream expressed in the art and the writing.

B. Somewhat connected with exercise A is dream journal construction. There are any number of ways to creatively design a dream journal. The journal can be personalized with art and with titles and categories for specific kinds of dreams, such as "My Dream and My Job" or "My Dream and My Life as a Student."

C. Dream dramatics is another way of linking dreams with oral skills and kinesthetic expression. For example, let us suppose a student had a flying dream in which she encountered various landscapes, buildings, people, animals, and other objects. She could put on a one-person show in which she reenacted the dream and conversed with each of the elements that appeared to her. You may also have class members role-play the elements of her dream as she arrived at them during flight.

Daydream Exercises

A. Have students face a window in the classroom. (If there is none, get a large piece of paper, draw one, and hang it in an appropriate spot on the wall.) Ask students to stare out the window in silence for a few minutes. Introduce the idea of becoming a butterfly that comes to the window and peers in at the class. Turn on soft music and ask questions about what the butterfly is doing, what it sees, how it feels, and what the world is like outside the window. Follow this exercise with writing (poetry, story, essay) and art.

B. Based on exercise A, have the students make life-size butterfly wings. Spare no expense, if possible, in supplying paints and necessary material to make the wings special. Find an open area and allow the children to do a butterfly dance, spontaneously improvising to a variety of music, from classical to rock. To extend the activity, the kids might script a brief scene involving two or three butterflies who meet in a garden or who get stuck in a butterfly net.

C. Blow up balloons for each student. So that they don't peek, have them put on blindfolds, then hand them one balloon each. Ask them to imagine what color their balloon is. Then have them daydream their balloon on a trip to all kinds of real and imaginary places. Begin background music. You can stop the music periodically to keep students from wandering too far. **Note:** Wandering is actually fine; it is the essence of daydreaming and can simply become part of the exercise. When finished, have students remove their blindfolds and share their journeys with one another. Like the other exercises, you can follow this exercise with writing, art, and dramatics.

Crocodile Dreams and Peach Pit Meanderings

Croc suggests to Peach Pit that they go for a flight anywhere, but that they put on the automatic pilot and drift through the skies for an unspecified length of time. With this suggestion Peach Pit is in full accord.

No sooner are they aloft, at what Croc referred to as "musing speed," than they leave the controls to Peach Pit's built-in energy system and whir quietly through the atmosphere without a care in the world.

The sun bathes Croc, gently massaging its way through his scales to his blood, which flows through his brain and soothes him into a deep sleep. Peach Pit trances out from the hummmmmm of its own propulsion. Two dreams float through the sky like packages of thought.

To his amazement Croc has dream-transferred to someone else's dream. The little boy whose dream he is now dreaming sits at his desk in Mrs. Grady's classroom while Mrs. Grady presents a wonderful lesson on geography and Kilamanjaro.

> *The tiger has climbed the wide, tall tree to a natural crotch where it divides into three fat, arced subdivisions that curve upward almost a hundred feet. In that crotch the boy sits as the tiger gently nests itself next to him as if it were simply a domestic kitten.*
>
> *"Who are you?" the boy asks the tiger.*
>
> *"I am 'Sendformeinyourdreams,' the tiger of youthful wisdom," replies the striped cat.*
>
> *"How did you find me?" asks the boy.*
>
> *"I didn't have to look. I just come when little kids are tired or when their brains need to rest from the logic of it all,"*

answers Sfmiyd. Croc is wondering if he will be noticed by either of them, tuned in as he is to the little boy's dream as if it were his own. His concern immediately becomes the center of attention.

"Someone is watching us," says Sfmiyd.

"I know," replies the little boy. Croc shifts his tail, hoping that he is not going to be kicked out of this dream.

"It's okay if he stays, but only if you don't mind," says the tiger.

"I don't mind," responds the boy, "but can we invite him to sit with us here in the tree?"

"I would say it is fine as long as he doesn't bite. Those crocodile teeth can hurt even big tigers like myself," says tiger matter-of-factly.

Croc is excited. Not only is he dreaming the same dream as the little boy, but he is going to receive an invitation to sit in the crotch of the tree with them as the dream continues. No sooner has he had the thought than he finds himself on the other side of the boy in the crevice of the tree.

"How are you, Croc?" asks the tiger. "This is your first dreamshare, isn't it?" Croc tells them that it is as the dream reveals itself.

The tiger leaps from the tree onto a big rock, motioning for the boy to follow. He does. Of course, at this point, Croc has no choice. It is his dream, too. So he jumps as carefully as a nonaerial creature as bulky as Croc can. The leap and the landing are quite smooth. The rock is hard, and all of its surface is a mirror.

"Oh, look, I can see myself in the rock," exclaims the boy. Moments pass and the rock grows into a buffalo roaming a large prairie with rolling hills and grass so green it seems like a large pool of broccoli.

"Get on my back, kid, and I'll get my friend Peach Pit to give us a boost so that we can keep up with that feline," suggests Croc.

The telepathic relationship Croc and Peach Pit share bring the little energy plant to them and off they fly behind the unpredictable dream tiger. They come to the edge of a canyon and don't stop for a second. The dream tiger looks back at them and says they can do anything as long as they keep the dream going and "for heavens sake don't wake up halfway across the canyon!"

Croc, Peach Pit, the boy, and the dream tiger float endlessly wherever their together-dream takes them. They tumble and bounce across a sky that forever changes its mix of colors, and everything shares in everything; nothing has a fixed definition; all things can fly, even whole forests. Croc notices something peculiar, however, as the dream begins to become disturbed and erratic, like a TV going on and off. He is losing contact with the boy. "Hey, Peach Pit, the kid is waking up or someone is waking him up!" says Croc.

"It's okay, Jimmy," says Mrs. Grady. "I'm sure your dream is more important." Croc returns to where his sleep began and wakes. Peach Pit stops humming and comes to his senses, too.

Memory

Jung (1965) tells us that his earliest memory was a vague one, "a rather hazy impression." He goes on to describe what is a pleasant recollection embedded in an experience during very early childhood.

"I am lying in a pram in the shadow of a tree. It is a fine, warm summer day, the sky blue, the golden sunlight darting through the green leaves. The hood of the pram has been left up. I have just awakened to the glorious beauty of the day, and have a sense of indescribable well-being. I see the sun glittering through the leaves and blossoms of the bushes. Everything is wholly wonderful, colorful, and splendid" (6).

Jung's description of his memory is presented in visual terms, for we usually think of memory as primarily visual. However, memory is a multisensory dimension. We remember texture, odor, taste, sound, and admixtures all at once.

One sensory remembrance triggers a memory stored as another sense. Recalling the hot sun on a beach may trigger recollection of thirst or the vision of ocean waves or the sound they made. The memories may be sequentially experienced or experienced simultaneously.

Memory is a fascinating power, for it seems that we forget nothing. Wilder Penfield uncovered this incredible fact while operating on epileptics. He stimulated various regions of the brain and his patients recalled experiences in detail, conversations verbatim, and voices so clear and perfect that the patients thought the people were present.

Not long after Penfield's work, biologist Karl Pribram discovered that memory is not necessarily localized, but is spread out across the whole brain like a hologram. This discovery has changed our model of what memory is as well as what learning is. We now feel more confident in asserting that both are associational by their very nature, that memory is coded by a connective tissue of related experiences, and that we learn analogically, that is, our brains associate data with other data to strengthen our knowledge of all data. In other words, everything is connected. Memory, therefore, becomes the model for holistic learning in which teachers make a conscious effort to simulate the associational activity of the brain (in the way they present content), anticipating this response. All content is interconnected and interdisciplinary in nature. Memory says this is so and so do our dreams and daydream fantasies.

Hungarian physicist-mathematician John von Neumann figured that the brain can store 280,000,000,000,000,000,000 bits of information (Talbot 1991, 21). In the work of Collier, Burkhardt, and Lin we discover that a one-inch square of film treated holographically can store more information than 50 bibles (Talbot 1991, 21).

Memory Activities

A. A good first activity would be to provide kids with a list of sensations that contain experiences they might have had. Based on one or two items chosen from the list, they attempt to describe the setting and time of the experiences and other things going on in their lives at the time. Following is a list of the kinds of things you might provide the students:

- sipping hot chocolate
- capturing a bug in a jar
- sand castles
- waiting for a phone call
- shining shoes
- taxicab rides
- jumping rope
- imitating someone

- raindrops falling on car windows
- the kitchen at Thanksgiving
- dirty hands you can't get clean
- diving under water with eyes open
- sore feet after a long walk
- Christmas stockings
- something crawling up your arm
- lying awake with eyes wide open
- hot fudge
- colorful clothing
- snow in the face
- the sock you forgot to put on
- things on top of your bureau
- the sound of water filling the tub
- the cold feel of something metallic
- coloring between the lines
- spilling your drink on the new tablecloth
- the taste of a green vegetable
- lawnmowers
- jumping into a pile of autumn leaves
- watching your breath on a cold day
- checking the ice to see if it's safe
- gargling
- soap in your eyes
- closing your eyes during a scary movie
- something you broke
- cooking sounds
- nose to the glass at the zoo

The secret to this activity is to avoid trying too hard to remember. Just make something up. More than likely it is going to be coming from some memory bank and some catalogued association. The freer and more wide open the response, the better.

B. A most enjoyable activity is discussing with secondary school students their memories of childhood. Sometimes it is good to guide the conversation to events you know from experience kids respond to, such as playground experiences, injuries and scraped knees, first pets, going to sleep at night, vacations, good friends, and so on. It is important to spend several hours recollecting and sharing these events that are embedded in their memories. Follow this activity by talking about free verse and then asking them to write a long free verse about their memories. When they are finished, have students read their poems out loud, then take questions from and discuss with the class.

> **Note:** To teach free verse familiarize yourself with e. e. cummings's poem "in just." Free verse is not ruled by conventional spelling and mechanics. It uses space between words, combines words, and accentuates the poet's freedom to find ways to use space and words to create image, metaphor, and meaning. To give a loose structure to the assignment you could require a certain minimum number of words as well as comparisons.

C. Create a memory time line showing a correspondence between historical events and historical anniversaries. For example, a fourteen-year-old student would first set up a month-by-month calendar from year one to the present. She would next fill in personal memories, a history of events in her life. Then she would research historical events that occurred at those times. Lastly, she would research other historical events that occurred in the past and that are celebrated yearly during that period on the time line. It is easy to use this exercise as a basis for writing, further research, journaling, artistic expression, and drama. Kids can share their time lines and develop various kinds of presentations that are a blend of autobiography and history.

Storytelling

There seems to be common agreement that the decline in storytelling (defined as an experience that is basically aural in nature) and the ascendancy of early childhood exposure to television (defined as a simultaneous visual-aural experience) are related. Critics of exposing children to large doses of television and computers claim that listening skills, creative imagination, and play are endangered.

Some claim that reading stories to children while they sit in your lap or snuggle up close to you makes them better readers at an earlier age. Others would modify this assertion by suggesting that the storybooks not be filled with pictures that offer a visual distraction from aural interpretation and use of the imagination.

Generally, the conclusions drawn boil down to the following: we are cultivating generations of children who are not capable of producing their own imaginary landscapes but rather reproduce landscapes provided by the media. Corollary inattentiveness to material presented only to the ear, as well as reduced imaginary play, result in increased school problems and loss of authentic self. These manifest themselves further in self-centered character development, which, in the extreme, is revealed in sociopathic behavior and disregard for others.

Are these observations true? There is probably some validity to them, but they might also prove to be overgeneralizations, because we are not fully aware of what is really going on with the media and children's minds. How much is too much simultaneous visual-auditory input? There probably is a point where it is too much, but there probably cannot be too much of the alternative. Therefore, the greatest assurance that the media's potential harm to children is held in check is to increase a child's experience of storytelling.

Anne Twitty (1986) tells us that many years after becoming familiar with a story, it came back to her. The story, "The Black Bull of Norroway," is about a girl who finds a bull instead of a prince for whom she is searching. The bull becomes for her a means of survival as she searches for the prince, who has been drugged by a witch. Eventually she finds her prince, who wakes from his stupor, the reward for the girl's many years of searching. Although the plot at first seems simply to be about romance, it is more about the discovery of meaning and hope. The Black Bull is one's power and courage to see through the darkness, to face disappointment (for the prince did not at first awaken to the girl's song), until "at last someone—you/I—chooses to pour out the drug that holds us in forgetfulness, knowing that Spirit sits and sings to a sleeping world. *He heard, and turned to her*" (16; emphasis in original).

Storytelling sticks and even beneath conscious awareness serves to pull things together, to help us make connections, without imposing a right answer to life's perplexing condition. Nancy Mellon (1992) in *Storytelling and the Art of Imagination* writes of storytelling as a fundamental skill of the Waldorf teacher. She states that, in perfecting this skill, part of the Waldorf approach to teaching, "I began to believe in earnest that storytellers have as profound a purpose as any who are charged to guide and transform human lives. I knew it as an ancient discipline and vocation to which everyone is called" (4). She goes on to say, "Is there any pain, sorrow, or nightmare too terrible to be told through a story? Are there fears and bewilderments too deep for a story to hold? Storymakers ultimately are devotees who accept all earthly feelings and carry them as wise children into the realms of joy" (6).

What, then, can we assert about storytelling as an important aspect of teaching and learning? The following make sense given what we know about the brain, and the development of imagination and creativity, individuality, play, and literacy:

1. Storytelling requires auditory channels for reception and visual personal creative imagination. These channels help develop listening skills as well as one's own authentic imagery to complete the story.

2. Storytelling allows children, teenagers, and adults to frame life's questions and possible answers to them in appropriately symbolic terms. Symbols operate on many levels to provide explanations that can be received by children of varying ages and abilities.

3. Storytelling creates community in the shared listening and the shared discussions that arise around the stories

4. Storytelling prompts writing, artwork, theatrics, dance, and thinking.

Storytelling Exercises

A. Begin with selections from *Aesop's Fables*. Review the "what" of the selection. Explore the "what about" carefully to avoid eliciting "right" answers. Have students create a parallel fable with different animals doing similar things. Share the fables and go through the "what" and "what about" responses. Based on this experience, have students create their own fables in which the animals behave in such a way that a lesson is taught by what takes place. Have students read their fables to the class. After the reading, the other students form questions about the fable for the storyteller to answer. Lastly, if the questions and answers have not already revealed the lesson, the class tries to decide what the story was intended to teach. When someone guesses correctly, that student reads his or her fable and the process continues.

B. Lights out. Play an episode of "The Shadow," the popular radio show of the 1940s in which the hero, Lamont Cranston, uses hypnotic powers to make himself invisible to criminals and thereby bring them to justice. At the end of the episode (about twenty to thirty minutes), lights go back on. Have students make a list of five moments from the broadcast they pictured clearly. Compare notes. Assign the students to teams of four to create their own "Shadow" radio show. When it is their turn to present their program, the team must have a flashlight to read from the script and each team member should occupy a corner of the classroom. Then: lights out; presentation is made; class lists and discusses most vivid scenes.

C. Slowly read "Rapunzel" from *Grimm's Fairy Tales*. When finished review the "what" of the tale and then discuss the "what about." Next hand out copies of "Rapunzel" from *Transformations* by Anne Sexton. Discuss the interpretation Sexton has placed on the fairy tale. Have students write an essay evaluating Sexton's transformation of the story. Lastly, have students create their own transformations of the tale, read them to the class, and discuss the twists they gave it.

Visualization and Guided Imagery

Two of the most important results of using visualization/guided imagery processes correctly follow:

1. Students may become more aware of their own authentic feelings and concepts.

2. Teachers come into contact with some of the best, most natural writing and art produced by their students.

For both students and teachers the evaluation of student work becomes a more pleasurable activity.

Visualization/guided imagery techniques have been slowly gaining acceptance in business, sports, medicine, and education. While we must be wary of exaggerated claims for its effectiveness in producing traditional learning results, that is, retaining factual and data-based knowledge, there does seem to be a much more legitimate connection with the motivational and affective framework of learning (Eastman 1993, 328).

The internal visual processes of the image-generating brain can activate vivid experiences. If you imagine yourself flying across the world, it is possible to feel as if this were truly happening. Therefore, writing and art that flow from this experience will have an authentic quality; the "authentic voice" will be tapped and expressed.

The levels of visualization and guided imagery vary from brief, close-the-eyes attempts to visualize something to more extended internal journeys. Here I emphasis the latter, for the body needs time to relax; entrainment with the flow of internal images takes time; and students need time to forget their immediate surroundings.

Preliminary Steps

Visualization/guided imagery journeys begin with the articulation of rules and methods to begin relaxing the mind and the body. *First,* explain to students that you are going to ask them to close their eyes to go on an imaginary trip. Afterward, they will be writing and creating art to describe their trip. Tell them that the most important rule is silence, because one person who decides to goof off ruins it for everybody. Add that they are not to force anything and, if they fall asleep, you will give them a copy of the journey so that without the benefit of the visualization they may still do the writing and the art.

Second, ask them to find a comfortable spot where they can close their eyes and not have to move around. Wait for all to find their spots; be sure all eyes are closed and there is silence. Tell them that you are going to help them get relaxed before the visualization begins.

Third, ask them to concentrate on their breathing, giving special note to the change in air temperature from cool inhale to warmed exhale. Ask them to concentrate on these temperatures and the gentle, natural rhythm of their breathing for about thirty seconds. Next ask students to concentrate on their heartbeat and to feel the pulse of this beat all over the body. Tell them it is like what happens when a rock is thrown into the middle of a pond; the ripples it creates flow to all the shore around the pond. When the heart beats it sends out ripples and pulses to the shoreline of the body, the skin. Ask students to concentrate on this pulse for about thirty seconds.

Fourth, tell them the journey is about to begin and that they should not struggle with the information you give them. Ask them to be attentive to the details their imagination provides. Then begin with the words, "In your mind's eye . . . "

Several Possible Journeys

Note that these journeys are interdisciplinary in nature. They can be used as part of an integrated curriculum or a more discipline-centered program. They have applications in language arts, art, science, math, social science, foreign languages, technical education, and even home economics and culinary arts. Here I suggest a few specific applications of the visualization/guided imagery journeys, but you will undoubtedly uncover many other possibilities. Also, you can adapt the following journeys to fit a particular grade level or situation.

Journey 1: The Dive

Read slowly and deliberately.

In your mind's eye imagine you are sitting in a boat with one other person, drifting out into the middle of a clear ocean. Behind you is a sandy beach with no people on it. Above you are the blue sky and a bright sun. In the air is the smell of salt water carried on a gentle breeze. Around you is blue-green water that is pure and teeming with fish, crabs, lobsters, and sea vegetation. Below is a treasure chest.

How do you feel? What do you clearly see? Are you ready to dive to the bottom where the treasure chest has been waiting for you to find it? What will the treasure chest look like? What do you imagine it contains?

See yourself move to the edge of the boat, carefully balancing yourself, aware that you will be swimming to depths that ordinarily require oxygen, but that you will be as comfortable in the sea as the fish who live there. At the edge of the boat your feet feel the hard surface from which you will take your plunge. Sunlight dances off the water and you dive. Your fingers cut the water first and your body follows. The water wraps you in cool stillness until a dolphin swims beside you, offering to be your aquatic taxi. You look straight into its eyes and telepathically say yes!

Holding on to the dolphin's back you plummet twenty feet to a sandy bottom, where fish of all sizes and shapes come to investigate you. Some come right to your body and swim along. Some come close and make abrupt U-turns away. A giant lobster moves like an old man across a rock covered in sea moss and varied-colored seaweed that is like hair blowing in a breeze; the seaweed moves with the current, hiding and revealing schools of small fish. You are amazed that breathing has not been a problem and you communicate to the dolphin that you want to go directly to the treasure chest.

The dolphin slows down as you approach the golden box that sits like a jewel on a sandy tablecloth. You release your grip on the dolphin and, alone, move the last five feet to the box as the dolphin waits for you. As you approach the box, the lid suddenly opens, and an intense shaft of light, as if from a powerful search beam, shoots straight up through the water and just as quickly loses brightness, leaving the box in a soft pinkish glow. You move to the edge of the chest and look in. There are five things in it, and a voice from within the box tells you that you may take only one. The five are a mirror, a watch, a smaller box filled with a million dollars, a bottle filled with a magic health elixir to cure all sickness, and a certificate that gives you the power to bring love and happiness to one needy person. The voice tells you to select wisely.

You feel confused but slowly make a decision about what it is you will take to the boat. You reach in and grab it. The dolphin moves close to you as the chest closes. The dolphin returns you to the bright surface of the ocean next to your boat. There is a person on board the boat to pull you aboard. Who is it? You find your spot on the boat and sit as the two of you silently begin the journey home. You are thinking many things.

Journey 2: The Painting

In your mind's eye imagine that you are sitting before a gigantic wall that is at least ten feet tall and thirty feet wide. It is clean and blank as new-fallen snow. In front of the wall on the floor are buckets of paint of every color imaginable. There are paint brushes of every size and shape. Imagine that whatever you want to paint, whatever you can see within your mind, you can paint on that wall.

You should also know that you will have the power to enter whatever scene you paint on the wall. Imagine yourself deciding what you are going to paint. Go over to the buckets of paint and carry the colors you want to use to the wall. Watch yourself select your brushes and begin to paint. What have you decided to paint?

Carefully watch the wall become what you are painting. Imagine that the wall is becoming exactly what you want it to become. If sounds are supposed to come from the scene you are painting, then hear those sounds. If you are painting a scene in nature and there should be smells coming from it, then smell the smells. Imagine that the odors are really there. If you would like, you can paint people and animals into the picture if they fit with your plans for the wall. Spend some time with the details and then step back from the wall to admire your work. Look at it and at every detail in the painting that has brought this wall to life.

You are now ready to enter the wall you have painted. Watch yourself step closer to the wall and stop right at the edge of the painting. Your next step will bring you into the scene you have painted on the wall.

You step slowly into the wall and find that your foot does not hit anything hard. You complete your first step and find yourself in your own painting, able to move around normally. Spend some time now in the scene you have painted. What are you going to do? What does it feel like? Looking out from the wall you can see the space from which you came, the space you were in when you painted the wall. What do you see? Are there any people there? If so, feel free to invite them into the wall painting. What is going on now? Spend a couple of minutes in the painting watching everything that you do and all the multisensory experiences that you have. (Pause for a minute or two.)

It is time to leave the painting, to step out from it into the space where the buckets of paint still rest on the floor. Watch yourself move to the edge of the painting and slowly step out onto the floor in front of the wall. How does it feel? Turn around and look at the wall. Do you want the scene to remain there or would you like it erased so you can paint another magical landscape?

Journey 3: Little Conversations

In your mind's eye imagine you are resting in a forest with your back against a tree and your eyes closed. You fall asleep as the warm sun gently soothes your face with its rays. "How do you like it here?" says a deep voice that seems to be coming from the tree. You answer. What do you say?

"Did you know that we trees know everything that goes on in the forest?" You answer. What do you say?

"It's nice when people like you stop here and lean against us for rest and relaxation," says the tree, "and it helps us to know how human beings are feeling. We can sense if they are sad or happy when they lean against us." The tree goes on to tell you how you are feeling. What does it tell you?

Your eyes are still closed and you are still asleep against the tree. See yourself so relaxed against this tree that has spoken to you and has become a friend. In your sleep you hear the sound of feet coming closer to you. A cold animal's nose sniffs your arm, but you do not awake. It is a deer.

"You look so peaceful and happy over here," says the deer. "You look like a friend to all the forest." In your sleep you respond to the deer. What do you say?

Still asleep, you feel a caterpillar crawl up your arm onto your face. In your mind's eye you see it crawl ever so slowly up to your left eye. It raises your eyelid and looks you straight in the eye and winks. It lets your eyelid down so that you can continue to sleep. Before leaving you, the caterpillar stops and says, "Dream on, dream on. Have the courage to live your dreams!" In your sleep you respond to the caterpillar. What do you say?

Gradually you open your eyes. In your back pocket there is a notepad and a pencil.

"Gonna write your dream, eh?" you hear the tree ask. You answer. You spend several minutes writing about your dream, not noticing that all the forest animals have gathered at your feet, watching you lovingly do your dream writing. You look up when you are finished and they are all there, smiling. Who is there? They begin to hum the most beautiful and peaceful sound you have ever heard. What does the humming sound like? How do you feel? What have you written? A bluebird flies to you and lands on your knee.

"They have asked me to bring you this message," says the bluebird. "We love you." You respond. What do you say?

You rise to your feet. There is a passage out of the forest. Do you leave or do you decide to continue to walk deeper into the forest?

Post-Visualization Steps and Activities

When the visualization is coming to an end, tell the students to open their eyes slowly. At this point there are several directions from which to choose.

1. the silent write/art response

2. the take a break, talk with your neighbor, get back to the silence write/art response

3. the discussion/silence/write/art response

Experiment with each to find which works best for you and your students. Following are suggestions for relating the activity to specific curriculum areas.

Language Arts and Art Activity

Either begin with a free-write about the visualization experience, asking the students to write about what happened and filling in all the details that their own minds added to the journey, or have them draw (or paint) a feeling or something connected with the trip. After that the writers should draw and the artists should write. Put the responses away for two days. After two days return to these initial responses, change them, refine them, and make final drafts of the written part. Students may also want to redraw or repaint. Choose a time to gather in a circle to share the art and the writing.

Science, Culinary Arts, Social Science Activities

Because the visualization/guided imagery experience is so real it provides an authentic and motivational backdrop for exploration in science, culinary arts, and social science. For example, in *science* these three journeys offer the opportunity for continued exploration into the ocean, into the nature of color, and into forest ecology and management. In *culinary arts* these journeys can be the basis for the study and use of herbs; catching, preparing, and cooking fish, lobsters, and crabs; finding out what goes into the preparation of an animal for eating, from the killing of the animal to its arrival on a dinner plate. In *social science* one can study the environmental movement and how it has and has not affected global political life.

Math and Technical Education Activities

Students can plot out a path through a forest, estimate the volume of water in a certain area of the oceans, or graphically plan a house to scale. They can create simulations of the journeys on computer and create audio-visual aids for a trip through a real forest near school or through a humanmade forest erected in a gym or an auditorium.

Foreign Language

Visualization/guided imagery conducted in a foreign language is a great opportunity for kids to link the visual and the verbal, and to begin thinking in the language itself. The foreign language teacher can rewrite each of these journeys or similar ones based on the level of the students. The journeys and the activities are conducted in the language.

Croc Has the Last Word, the Last Image

"Very interesting, very interesting!" comments Croc when he listens to Peach Pit humming about all this visualization stuff. "I liked the ocean thing. I picked out the money. I mean, c'mon, who's gonna be stupid enough to pick anything else? The money can get you any of the other four things. That was an easy one.

I liked meeting some of my aquatic brethren and sistren. That was cool!

"I painted a large rock sticking out of a swamp on a sunny day. I walked into the wall and perched on that rock all day. What a life!

"The forest was another story, Peach Babe, it was so difficult not to open my eyes and eat a few of the animals, but I stayed with the flow there."

Peach Pit hums and Croc knows it is time to fly. Croc walks to the buckets of paint that are still on the floor by the gigantic wall. He paints a sky full of rainbows, and no two are the same array of colors. In a flash, like a match struck in darkness, Croc and Peach Pit are off into the painting, into the sky full of color, leaving a streak of vapor behind them.

4

Art and Abstract Designs across the Curriculum

Today we hold a stone, the heavy stone of power. We must perceive beyond it, however, by the aid of the artistic imagination, those humane insights and understandings which alone can lighten our burden and enable us to shape ourselves, rather than the stone, into the forms which great art has anticipated.

—Loren Eiseley

What would happen if all curriculum began as art? Let us imagine several starting points in a number of disciplines.

Science

We begin with a picture of the heart followed by color slides that clearly show the heart from every angle. The students first draw the heart from memory and then from a series of pictures. Next, the students make a three-dimensional clay heart. Finally, each student takes Polaroids of all their hearts. Only then do they learn anatomical data, names, and functions. From this starting point each student then constructs a human body or the body of a life form that possesses a heart.

Social Science

Students begin by building a city from various materials. Next students draw or paint the city on canvas in water color or oils. Then students take Polaroids of the cityscapes. Only then do teachers and students begin to discuss what makes a city, how they come to be, and the problems and benefits of city life. Students form teams and build dream towns that they exhibit, describe, and answer questions about.

Mathematics

Students begin with still-life painting, followed by creating designs that have only one rule: they must be symmetrical. Then students attempt to develop fractal patterns by using special software programs now available for computers. When these are finished, students may discuss and discover the mathematical structures, geometries, trig functions, algebraic forms, simple number distributions, and quantitative patterns and probabilities within the designs. Students follow this discussion and discovery by creating math textbooks that reflect this process.

What has happened in each of these cases is very exciting, grounded in personal artistic expression, and built upon a reference point that is both concrete and symbolic. It is concrete because it can be sensed. It is symbolic because it contains quantitative and qualitative meaning that can be discovered and articulated. What would happen if art became an integral part of reading and writing?

Abstract Designs as Artistic Starting Points

The use of imagery extends to the creation of designs. Designs are all around us and influence the way we think and feel. Fashion design is a good example, but design extends into everything we do and permeates our sensory world. We design cars. We design homes. We design everything that goes into a home. We design layouts in stores. We design the way things are packaged. All of these designs have symbolic value to us. They represent ideas, values, and goals. They cloak meaning.

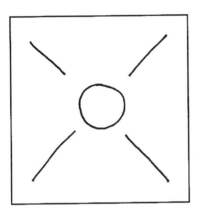

The design at left could represent the noun-idea of *decision*. The circle, alone in an empty space, sees before itself several roads and must decide which one to take. It is a time for decision!

Design making is a whole-brain activity because it *merges the visual and the verbal* to elicit meaning from students as they ponder what they have read or written. Designs stimulate reading and writing that are thoughtful, authentic, and valued. You can provide students with designs to work from or have students create their own.

The level of thought needed to use designs in the curriculum is high in Bloom's taxonomy—analytical and synthetic reasoning. This high level of thought has the added and necessary blessing of coming from the authentic voice of a student. Two fundamental levels of thought are kicked into gear when students are engaged in reading, writing, drawing, and living. These are the *literal* and the *symbolic*.

Literal interpretation points to what is physically present. A literal interpretation of the above design is the statement that "the design is the picture of a circle in an empty space near a bunch of lines going in outward directions." The interpretation here is simply a verbal mirroring of the physical arrangement of two forms.

Symbolic interpretation (also called metaphor, theme, and analogy) is an explanation of the design as a representation of an abstract idea. The idea represented above is *decision*. Symbolic interpretation goes beyond the literal, realistic representation. It connects the design to a world of ideas, themes, and categories. Although our goal is symbolic interpretation, literal interpretation is a worthy and excellent stepping stone toward the symbolic.

In fact, literal interpretation is sometimes no less perceptive than the symbolic. It may be one thing to know what eyeglasses symbolize, but it is best to see them on one's face first.

Higher-Order Thinking Skills

Design making challenges students to develop an intelligent pattern of thinking that taps their *analytical* and *intuitive* minds. Design making requires neural circuits to work together across the hemispheres more intensely than they ordinarily would.

Designs should be used at all levels of age and ability. Once the activity is established as part of your classroom repertoire—for interpreting reading material and stimulating writing—you'll be amazed at the higher-order thinking skills that design making encourages. Young children, slow learners, children with special needs, gifted and talented children—all students—will achieve some very interesting interpretations in either the literal or abstract and symbolic realms.

Specific Uses of Design Making

1. The Chart of Supplied Designs

Create a chart of designs to introduce students to design making as an integral part of reading and writing. On page 79 is an example of such a chart.

When making your own chart, be sure to draw it on a large piece of paper (about 3 feet by 3 feet) and place it on a wall for all to see. Leave it there for several days before introducing it to allow students to absorb the designs and begin to make connections beneath their conscious awareness. Your students will probably ask you about the chart, because it will draw their curiosity.

The *first activity* using the chart involves asking the students to do one of the following: (a) pick out one of the designs that reminds them of something and explain in writing; (b) pick out a design that represents how they feel and explain in writing; (c) pick out a design that represents them as a person and explain in writing. In directing students in this activity, be sure to tell them that whatever design they choose to write about will be their

design and however they explain it will be correct. There is no right or wrong way to explain their choices.

After you collect the papers on which students have copied their designs of choice and provided explanations, you will notice that some students tend to be literal and others tend to be abstract, symbolic, or metaphoric in their descriptions. These papers will give you information that indicates students' developmental level of thinking.

2. Using Supplied Designs for Reading Comprehension

Select a story the students can follow as readers but which you will read to them in *two installments*. After you have read the first installment, have students select a design from the Chart of Supplied Designs to represent the story to that point. Ask that each student copy their chosen design and explain why the design connects to or represents the story.

You might want to have each student share with the class what design was selected and why in order for the whole class to experience various interpretations latent in the designs. These explanations will also give you more evidence about the levels of thinking in the class.

Later or when you are next with the group, finish the story. Ask each student to pick a second design to represent the now completed story and to explain why the design was selected. Add to the request the following question: What did the second design have that the first design didn't to help interpret the story? Students who prefer to continue using the first design should explain why; that is, what new information did the student get out of the first design once the story was completed?

This exercise reinforces the link between the visual and the verbal as tools for reading comprehension and adds the skill of comparing and analyzing the differences between the two designs.

Of course all the activities involve *discussion* and the integration of designs to foster reading comprehension. There is another built-in activity: *conferencing*. Because of the involved nature of visual interpretation, student-teacher dialogue is deepened, especially in the conference format. You can ask many questions of the student with the designs as the focal point. Help students explore why they selected their designs and what other designs from the chart might be used to interpret the story.

3. Students Create Their Own Designs

Because the class is composed of students at different thinking levels (literal and symbolic), the first time you ask students to create their own designs to represent the story, stress that you would like them to make designs that *represent* the story but are not drawings of objects from the story.

You will find that students who are very much at the literal level will draw something literally from the story. Tell them that you'd prefer a design as opposed to a drawing of something in the story, but that their work is acceptable and their grade won't be lowered. Assure them that eventually they'll know and see the difference and not to be the least concerned. With certain students this reassurance may have to be repeated until their trust in you solidifies.

You can also have students create designs (similar to the Chart of Supplied Designs) to be used in activities. It would be helpful to keep in a notebook this process of reading followed by design selection or design creation and explanation. This notebook will enable you and your students to keep track of the evolution of levels of thought. Once students get into this process, you might be amazed at the progress, insight, and levels of abstract thought that even the most literal of thinkers can develop.

4. Designs + Theme Words + Explanation

At some point you will want to take the process a bit more directly to the symbolic/abstract level by introducing *theme words* or what can also be called *noun-ideas*. Here is one effective way to set up this activity:

1. Inform students that you are going to help them develop a skill that is not only important in reading comprehension but also in the understanding the meaning of life itself; tell them that the skill of being able to see *themes* in reading and in life is important because it helps one understand the real *issues* raised by literature and living.

2. Give students an example by telling them an abbreviated, homemade version of a "chicken crossing the street" story. Tell them that the chicken failed to look both ways and was flattened by a truck. Ask the class to tell you what the story was about and what the central theme was. Some will give you the theme in terms of a moral, such as "Be careful and always look both ways before you cross a street." At some point ask the class to represent their response in one word. You might get suggestions like "stupidity," "death," or "carelessness." These words are nouns and also central themes or ideas in the story.

3. Tell another chicken tale in which other themes are embedded. If you get an adjective such as "funny," help the student transpose it into a noun equivalent, such as "humor" or "fun." After a while you will have developed a large list of noun-ideas that you can display on a poster in the classroom. Here is a sample list of noun-ideas/themes (in alphabetical order):

addiction	nothingness
beauty	opulence
creativity	play
death	quiet
embarrassment	rebellion
freedom	sex
greatness	teasing
health	understanding
influence	violence
journey	winning
kindness	youth
love	zeal
masculinity	

4. At this point the class is ready to combine designs and noun-ideas in their reading comprehension. As with other activities, try to find a suitable story that can be read either aloud or silently. Ask the class to (1) choose or create a design to represent the theme of the story, (2) write down the noun-idea/theme word that the design represents, and (3) explain why the design represents the theme word of that story.

When students have finished, everyone in the class will be doing some degree of thinking at the abstract, symbolic level, even the most literal minded of students. To them this elevation of their thinking level will not seem forced and they will not be urged to so something for which they are not developmentally ready. For some students, their designs may still be quite literal or realistic, but their explanations will be a bit more abstract because the intention is to analyze thematically.

5. Designs and the Writing Process

There are several ways to integrate design drawing and writing.

- ◆ Use the designs as a starting point, as in the previous exercises in which the design is the intermediary between reading and writing.

- ◆ Use the designs to represent a feeling or a reminder of something personal.

- ◆ Use the design making as part of the early brainstorming of the writing process (where the designs, as opposed to an outline, give rise to an essay). The designs become a free-flowing visual expression of feelings and ideas not evident to students until they study the finished piece and begin to write.

- ◆ Use the designs as an integral part of keeping a diary in which the designs become a kind of visual piñata stuffed with the words that will fill the pages of the diary.

6. The Design, Theme, and Writing Project

The following integrated visual-verbal project, which was created for tenth-grade language arts students, is fundamentally appropriate at many grade levels. You can adapt the activity to suit your needs.

The project involves having students create twenty to thirty designs, interpret the theme of each design through a noun-idea word, and then explain the connection between the theme and the design.

Several students found it difficult to produce the required number of designs. They needed reassurance that they were doing fine. Several discovered that the suggestion to create the designs freely and spontaneously unblocked them, because they became free from the pressure to make immediate sense out of things. Once they abandoned that pressure, the designs just flowed and so did their writing.

Some loved the project because it was visual. (Conservative estimates say that 30 to 40 percent of students are visual learners.) The project for them was also challenging and helped them discover the joy of writing. Writing, as it was connected to the design interpretation, took on a new feeling, the sensation of authenticity. For many students, writing had lost that personal and expressive quality, and this project unearthed for them deep satisfaction in the writing process.

Other students loved the project primarily because of the design making, and they produced some of the most unusual, beautiful, and intricate designs among their peers. Their written explanations were excellent as well, since they were motivated to do verbal justice to their designs.

Lastly, there were the designs of the more literal-minded thinkers, who broke through much of their literalness and stretched themselves into the symbolic realm without having their thought processes violated.

Student Examples

The following are examples from among the hundreds that were handed in for the project; by them you can calibrate levels of thinking and see how a variety of students handled the verbal-visual process. Level 1 refers to the *literal* level and level 2 refers to the *symbolic* level.

1. **Amicability**

Explanation: "To me this picture represents amicability because this design looks so peaceful, and it does not look like it can hurt anything. The triangle connects to the tree which enables the tree to be stable, and not to go outward and hurt anyone or anything."

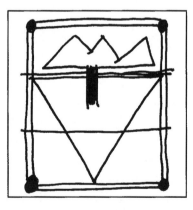

About the Student: DB came to my level 2 class halfway through the year. He was intelligent but sanguine and choleric in temperament (see the works of Rudolph Steiner for an exploration of the four temperaments) and, therefore, easily distracted. In addition he was used to whining and making excuses for poor reading and writing skills, neither of which was really poor. By the end of the term he had discovered his real abilities and was fairly fluent in the visual-verbal process. His design is partly abstract and partly literal, especially since his forms are easily identifiable as objects—the triangle and the tree—yet together they have an abstract quality, which he expressed in his noun-idea and written explanation.

2. Love

Explanation: "This picture is a symbol of love because it represents a person's intense affection for another based on familial or personal ties. When you love something you usually have your full attention on that one person and you usually spend most of your time with this person."

About the Student: JR had a lot of difficulty graduating to the symbolic level and was often frustrated in her attempts to draw simply designs and not real objects. When she finally broke through, she smiled and said, "Oh, I get it now!" She produced one of the most cared for projects in the class. You will note that while her noun-idea for the design is *love,* it could easily have been *intensity* or *attentiveness,* forms of which appear in her explanation.

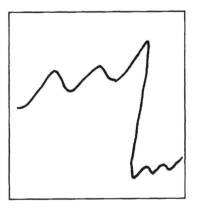

3. Stock Market

Explanation: "When I look at this drawing I see our stock market as a bull then dropping to a bear market. One day comes to mind and that is October 29, 1988, when there was a stock market crash. Luckily nobody killed themselves like in the one back in the 20s. The stock market is a tricky game. It made millionaires and poor people that have no money."

About the Student: KA was in my class only a quarter of the year and did not really graduate to the abstract, symbolic level, although I have no doubt he would have. A coded kid, he had some perceptual problems that required multisensory approaches as well as confidence building. KA's example is a good one because you can see the literal relationship between the visual, the theme (which is not abstract but rather a place name), and the explanation. It would not take him long to see that a theme word might be something like *fate, unpredictability,* or *fluctuation* and his explanation would have referred to the stock market crash simply as an example, but not as a focus of the piece.

4. Choice

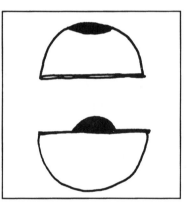

Explanation: "The two half circles in this picture represent choice. The two half circles are identical except for where the dark colored area is placed. They are placed in different places because it shows that it was their choice where they wanted it placed and that it is okay to be different."

About the Student: AC was a quiet, level 1 girl who liked designs that were simple and could be used for many possible basic themes and direct, uncomplicated explanations.

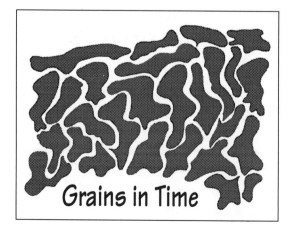

5. Time

Explanation: "This picture reminds me of grains in time because each little piece represents a time in life. To me this picture represents little pieces of time coming together in one big life and time in any relationship. Time is connected with me because relationships are connected with time. Time is what makes a relationship work."

About the Student: TP came to my level 3 class as a highly intuitive underachiever, easily discouraged by past failure. She flourished in my class and found the visual-verbal work to be inviting, challenging, and enjoyable. It became evident to me that she was a very bright girl.

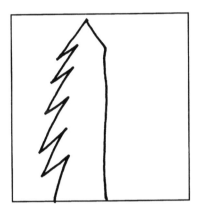

6. Difference

Explanation: "This picture represents that on one side this is part of a Christmas tree. On that side people love Christmas and love to spend money. And on the other side there is nothing just a straight line and on that side people hate Christmas and don't spend money."

About the Student: TE was a literal type in a level 3 class. He had major problems organizing his thoughts and shaping what he had to say. The visual-verbal process gave him an opportunity to think about representing his thoughts in a connected and organized manner.

7. Balance

Explanation: "Balance is a ratio of two or more things. It can be just the right amount of spin-to-force on a horseshoe. It could be the right amount of acid-to-base. There is one thing that doesn't change, and that is that balance is always the perfect ratio to accomplish each goal. Balance cannot exist without imbalance.

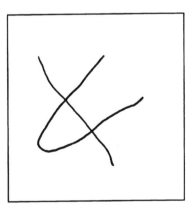

If everything were in perfect synch, harmony and balance, what would we strive for? You can't right a nonexistent wrong.

About the Student: BJ was a level 1 student whose drawings were basic but whose explanations were marvels of philosophical insight. I spent a lot of time exploring with him the explanation for this design. Our conversation brought us into the notion of chaos theory and thus caused him to add the last sentence to his explanation.

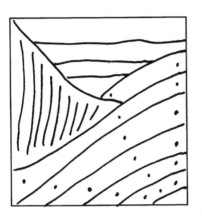

8. Secrets

<u>Explanation:</u> "I think this shows secrets as each dot being a new secret in someone's life, and the darker part covering them up hiding them from everyone. People have secrets because some things you just can't share."

<u>About the Student:</u> GS, a level 2 student, stated that this project helped him to like and enjoy writing and to see for the first time that writing had a purpose, to express oneself, one's feelings, and one's real thoughts. Up to that time he was restricted by approaches to writing that were too structured and showed little interest in what we call "authentic voice."

9. Acceptance

<u>Explanation:</u> "All the shapes and colors are different, but they accept each other. They come together to form one beautiful form and they don't treat each other differently. The shapes cooperate together and they like each other as they are. That is the best acceptance in the world."

<u>About the Student:</u> TJ, a level 1 student, really experimented with forms and easily drew from them great ideas and excellent explanations. When she was working on her original draft she would sit in deep thought, entertaining multiple possibilities for both her drawings and their symbolic meanings. At times she'd spontaneously talk or exclaim out loud when she was pleased or surprised by what she discovered in her own work.

10. (No theme words selected)

Explanation: "This is about a flock of birds that come across a magical prairie. In their majestic flight they land with smoothness and grace. The words themselves have a peace, a freedom and a beauty within them."

11. (No theme words selected)

Explanation: "These words express the vast universe that we inhabit. It tells you of the mighty wonders that every planet plays in the system. How everything around us has their own musical notes that make the universe a vast and mysterious place to live. Each little thing in this universe sings a special song. A song that holds everything in place, the song that keeps us all together in this Universe."

About the Student: KP (level 3) was one of those psychic/intuitive persons who is sparked by an activity, releasing enormous universal insights and connections, without necessarily fulfilling all the goals of the activity. KP's drawings tended to be elaborate, literal, and also surreal. He never settled on a theme word but rather titled his drawings in phrases, some literal and some abstract. His explanations were penetrating and often cosmic. The activity thoroughly engrossed KP. He became frustrated only when his feelings and words didn't quite match. When he realized it was best not to dwell too long on one design when the words weren't coming, he learned to shift to another or to just put the activity down for a while.

12. Destiny

Explanation: "This design is made mostly of triangles, which have three sides. The three sides of the triangles represent the past, the present and the future. All three are determining

factors in our destiny. The black triangle at the bottom center represents all that is known. The two semi-3D triangles in the upper corners represent things from the past coming together with things in the present and on into the future."

<u>About the Student:</u> JW (level 2) has purposely been left as the last student example. The full catalogue of his designs and noun-idea words follow. JW became completely drawn into the design-making process to such an extent that the designs took on a beauty, style, and aesthetic quality all their own. When JW finished he had no preconceived notion about what they meant. In this respect he was doing the project as it was originally intended, that is, to abandon oneself to the design making and to later discover the themes (archetypes) in each. JW discovered a great deal in his designs and fleshed out verbal explanations that were insightful, interesting, and vivid proof of the incredible minds that kids possess and reveal when the visual and the verbal are creatively united in an activity.

The Remainder of JW's Designs

What follows are JW's designs and the themes he associated with them. A teacher might use these designs to enrich the chart of supplied designs or as a backlog from which to create alternative design-based activities.

Helplessness

Peace

Seasons

Temptation

Aggression	Suffering	Space	Personalities
Stress	Annoyance	Faith	Fantasy
Life	Laughter	Energy	Discovery
Heaven	Nature	Feelings	Aging
Delicacy	Religion	Joy	Confusion
Birth	Pain	Evil	Magic

7. The Extended Essay or Report and Other Genres

When the designs, theme words (or phrases), and explanations are completed, the work thus far can become the basis for a more focused, specific, and developed piece of writing. The *essay* itself develops the expressed theme by branching out from the theme to its corollary ideas as well as applications and examples. Webbing or clustering an outline would be an excellent visual-verbal extension of this whole-brained approach.

A *story* might use the design in at least two ways. First, the characters, plot, and settings would all be woven together to express the theme. Second, the design would appear in the story and have some central importance to the plot; for example, it might be found on display in an art museum, an antique shop, or someone's home.

A *play* would utilize it the same way as a story.

Poetry can be derived from the theme or attempt (in free verse or rhyme) to describe either the design itself or provide a self-conscious commentary on the utility of designs and art in education.

A *research paper* might use the design as a starting point. If the design theme is "success," then the research paper can focus on the elements necessary for becoming successful as well as examples of people who have put these elements together to produce their own success stories.

A *letter* is another superb written way to extend the use of the design. For example, the student could pretend he or she had received the design as a gift from a friend or a close relative and is motivated to write a thank-you letter in which observations about the design are made.

8. A Teacher Workshop

An individual teacher or group of teachers who collaborate and conduct their own in-service programs can use what follows to get to know this powerful tool for teaching. In a group, allow two hours, because discussion and comparisons are important.

A. The "Maluma and the Tuckatee"

In order to establish the relationship between word and image, select which shape of the following you would name "Maluma" and which shape you would name "Tuckatee."

Figure A   **Figure B**

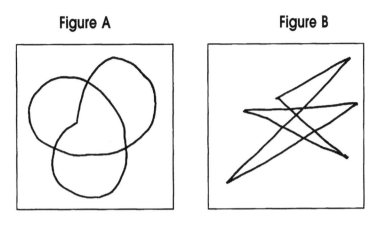

DO NOT READ FURTHER UNTIL
YOU HAVE MADE YOUR SELECTIONS.

W. Kohler, Gestalt psychologist, presented this task to his subjects. All connected "Maluma" to Figure A and "Tuckatee" to Figure B. It should be noted that Morton Hunt used this task in his book *The Universe Within* to demonstrate "the ability of the average person to make metaphorical-analogical connections between very unlike areas of experience" (Hunt 1982, 292).

B. Literal and Metaphorical Minds

Next, to establish the basic difference between literal and metaphorical association between a design and words and thoughts, describe what the following design is literally and what it might be symbolically or metaphorically.

<u>Literal</u>   <u>Metaphorical</u>

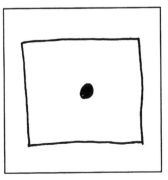

C. Getting Personal with the Designs

From the following five designs select the one that best symbolizes who you are and explain it in at least twenty-five words.

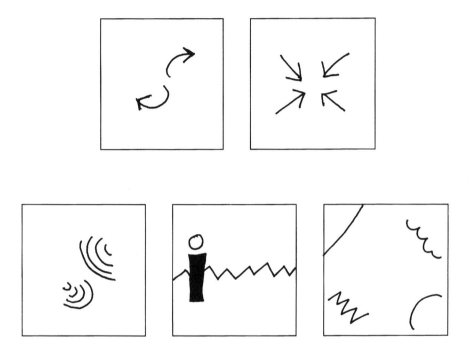

D. The Chart of Supplied Designs, Storytelling, Design Selection, and Reading

From the Chart of Supplied Designs select the one that best represents a story. **Note:** If you do this activity with a group of teachers, have the group first read the same story. After selecting the design, they copy it and explain why it was chosen to represent the story.

E. The Theme (Noun-Idea) and the List of Themes (Noun-Ideas)

At this point, small groups brainstorm theme words (which must be nouns) that are connected to the design below to get teachers used to connecting theme nouns to designs.

F. Writing, Creation of Own Designs, Theme Ideas and Explanation

This activity is the final step to introduce teachers to the process. It has the following steps:

1. Each creates own design.

2. Write a story, poem, or essay based on that design.

3. Select a theme noun that represents the design and the story.

4. Explain how the design contains the theme as expressed in the story.

9. Integrating Computers into the Process

English teacher Carolyn Yates, who took one of my workshops on design making and the curriculum, has put together a lesson plan for designs created on computer. The lesson flows from the reading of Hemingway's *The Old Man and the Sea.*

You can assign the procedure at any stage of the narrative; however, more options open up as the story nears completion. A handout with facts about Hemingway accompanies the lesson.

You need a classroom computer with one station if a network is not available. You will need drawing and word processing software. The first designs can be as simple as those that follow:

Design A   **Design B**

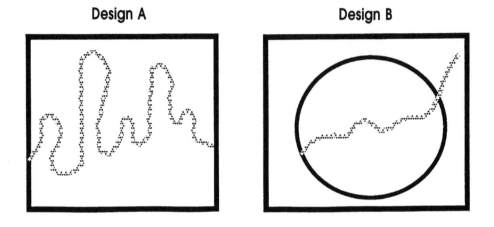

Design A could be an example of the "ups and downs" that a character might have within the story. It might also be used to represent "deception," the false trail a character leads detectives on in a mystery story. **Design B** cold have the same meanings as long as they can be justified by their connection to the character or the plot.

Students should master the steps for working with the program so that you can be free to wander around the classroom to help or to respond to individual needs and ideas. The steps for working with ClarisWorks are as follows (other programs might be similar):

1. Turn on the computer.

2. Input discs for ClarisWorks or click on ClarisWorks icon on the hard disc.

3. Click on the drawing program of ClarisWorks when the program directs you to.

4. The screen will display a page with grids and a series of tool palette options on the left of the screen.

5. The pointer will access the drawing tools; the letter "A" will enable the creator to use the word processing program on the drawing page.

6. Click on the rectangle tool, then select an area on the grid. Hold down the option key and move the cursor on the grid until the design is the size you want. You have drawn a square.

7. The corners of the design will be highlighted. If the size and shape do not meet your needs, click on one of the corners and adjust it.

8. Now select a border for the square from the menu options at the bottom of the palette. The line thicknesses are numbered and are reproduced on the screen so that the outline will help you stay in the controlled space as you continue your design.

9. After you have created the square, experiment with the design options available on the tool menu; all that is needed is your imagination and a steady hand on the mouse.

10. When you are satisfied with your design, from the file menu ask the computer to save your design and give your design a file name.

Students must look critically at their designs and make connections with the story. They should use the word processor on the computer and write a paragraph with their explanations. They should name this new document. The two (design and explanation) will be merged later.

Creating a document that contains both the design and the explanation is a simple process:

1. Decide where on the page you will place the design.

2. From the file menu select "new." The menu will ask if a word processing or drawing file is needed; select word processing.

3. Return to the file menu and select "open." Choose the drawing file containing the design. When the file appears on screen, choose "select all" from the edit menu.

4. Copy and paste. The design will appear on the page at the cursor position.

5. Move the cursor to the section where the explanation is to be added. Repeat the procedure, selecting file, open, select all, copy, paste. Give the document a new name.

Croc Teaches Peach Pit a Design

"Peach Pit, come here!" calls Croc, almost leaping out of his lizard skin.

"Leaping lizards, Croc, what's the big deal, man?" responds Peach Pit.

"Look at the design I've scratched into this rock with my front baby tooth that never fell out," commands Croc.

"What is it, Croc?" asks Peach Pit.

"It's what I'm all about. It's what an intelligent, curious, wondering, experimental, inquisitory, searching, humble, and generous Croc is all about!" proclaims Croc.

"Ahem, I don't want to burst your croc-o-bubble, but all I see is confusion, Croc, confusion and indecisiveness and uncertainty and vagueness and puzzlement and a kind of ignorance," says Peach Pit.

"Yes, and those, too," remarks Croc with a look of satisfaction.

With that Peach Pit starts up the engines, Croc climbs aboard, and they dart faster than light into the intelligent, curious, wondrous, experimental, inquisitorial, searching, humble, generous, confusing, uncertain, and puzzling universe.

5

The Enhancement of Learning through Sound

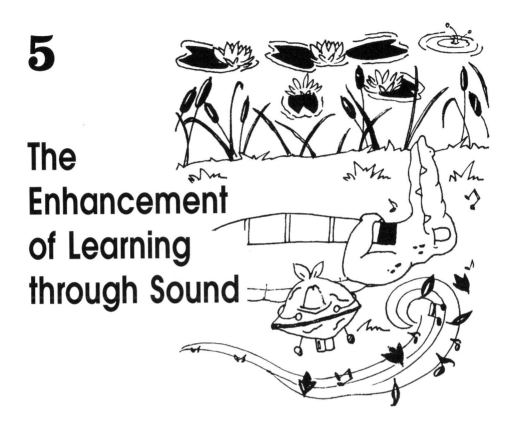

The hills are alive with the sound of music.
With songs they have sung for a thousand years
The hills fill my heart with the sound of music.
My heart wants to sing every song it hears.

—Richard Rodgers

The word *sound* has several different meanings with different roots. The human ear processes sound waves between fifteen cycles and twenty thousand cycles per second. However, when we use such phrases as "getting a sound education" or "sounding out his views," we use versions of *sound* with two different roots, *soun* and *sund*. Yet these roots share the same cognate, *un*, whose meaning is connected to water. We are left with the fascinating question: Is *sound* somehow connected with *water* in its evolution as a word? Additional information raises a second question: Are creation myths somehow connected to both water and sound?

From Christian creation stories we get "In the beginning was the Word." In Eastern religions we find *Om*, the sound of creation.

In most creation stories we also find some form of water, be it rain, ocean, or sea. There is a sense that the world is a cosmic embryo floating in a sea of emptiness connected by vibratory waves of information. Indeed, this world mirrors the reality of the human embryo floating in a sea of fluid in a world of vibrations, not the least of which is sound.

Richard Rodgers expressed more than he intended when he wrote those glorious lines quoted at the beginning of this chapter. The world is alive with the sound of life. Sound is evidence of life from the first cry of a baby to the last gasp at death. Laughter and lachrymae are states of emotional sound. Climate is a sounding out of both the quantity and temperature of water in a region. We live in weather that is cold or hot, wet or dry. Always there is a reference to water. Air and water are fluids. Sound, therefore, is the evidence of life in the water.

Through multiple uses of sound we learn for better or worse, we feel better or worse physically and psychologically, and we can create environments conducive to balanced human relationships and the development of community. When people are free to really sound each other out, to sound off, and to share some sound advice, they are creating community. Being aware of sound teaches a teacher a great deal. The biggest lesson it invites us to learn is the wisdom of the word as it exists in every living thing.

Sound must be accompanied by listening, for listening is a form of obedience to the true sound of life. By listening we learn to obey our hearts and we enter the true rhythm of life. We develop sound minds in sound bodies. For this reason we begin our journey of the evolution of a sound mind in the sound body of our mother, in the womb.

Alfred Tomatis (1991) asserts that "communication of sound is the most important link between a mother and a child within her. Once she has given it a nest within herself, she nourishes it in every way, especially with sounds. She reveals herself to the fetus by all the organic and visceral noises she makes and, above all, by her voice. The infant is steeped in this environment of sound. It draws all its emotional material from its mother's voice" (127). Therefore, both from nurture and nature perspectives, sound ought to be a top priority when educators plan their curricula, set up their classrooms, build their schools, and enter relationships with one another and the students they serve.

We are swimming in a sea of sound. Understanding that sea must be considered a basic requirement for teachers. Using sound must be considered a basic teaching skill, whether it be the use of one's teaching voice, the use of music, the use of recordings of nature's emanations, the use of student voices, the use of movement and voice as in exercise and drama, or the use of sound awareness in general.

The Sound in the Image/ The Image in the Sound

The two activities that follow illustrate the importance of sound. The first activity, "Guided Imagery with a Focus on Sound," focuses on images whose main purpose is to mentally evoke their sounds so that one has a sensation of their presence within the auditory system of the brain. The second activity, "Guided Sound with a Focus on Imagery," focuses on sounds whose main purpose is to give rise to images. Because all systems are interrelated, images give rise to sound, sound to images, both to tactile sensation, and so on.

Guided Imagery with a Focus on Sound

You can use the following activity at most grade levels. You may need to adapt it to suit your students. It possesses a dual sensory purpose: to evoke visual and auditory experience. In addition to its primary sensory function, it is intended to help students write, converse, and share with one another.

Begin by relaxing the students. A good way is to have them simply close their eyes, focus on their breathing, and let go of any concerns they might have. When they are ready, begin the journey, which we shall call "The Inner Ear." Read slowly and pause deliberately.

The Inner Ear: Part 1

Imagine yourself in a tub that is filling with water. The sound of the water rushing out of the faucets fills the bathroom. You duck your head under the water to hear the filling tub. It sounds different, much calmer, peaceful.

You turn off the water. The faucets squeak a bit. The tub becomes calm. You decide to drain the water. You duck your head again to listen as the water leaves the tub. You keep your head under until the water suddenly drops beneath your ears. It all sounds different now.

There is a window next to the tub. It is summer. The window is open, but you are protected from bugs by a screen. A bee flies to the screen and leaves. You concentrate and think you can hear it as it returns to its hive in the woods nearby. You look out the screen and scratch your fingernails along it, listening to the grating sound it makes. In the trees birds chirp and squirrels make their "tsuh-tsuh" sounds. One runs across the grass and climbs up the screen window. You hear yourself say, "Well, hello there, how are you today, squirrel?" It leaps from the screen to the ground where a nut lies. The squirrel picks up the nut in its front paws and begins to eat it. You can hear the nut being chewed. It makes you hungry.

Leaving the bathroom, you walk to the kitchen. Your slippers slide across the floor. They sound like the palms of your hands being rubbed together. You hear bacon frying, sizzling like raindrops hitting the roof of your house. The refrigerator is humming. You open the door and pull out the carton of eggs. You hear the door close as you carefully rest the carton on the kitchen counter.

After opening the carton, you carefully raise an egg to your ear. You listen. From inside the egg you hear what seems to be the sound of bubbles followed by a big burp. You hear yourself laugh and in the moment of laughter you drop the egg to the floor. You hear it crunch and splash open, and you screech, "Oh, no!" But from the egg steps a small self-playing marching drum, drumming a loud and fast beat that makes you laugh and want to march. So you line up behind the drum and you both march through the house with heavy and noisy footsteps that wake up the dog and cat, who begin barking and hissing at the strange sight of the little marching drum. Amid the drumming, footsteps, barking, and hissing, suddenly there is the sound of alarm clocks going off as everyone wakes up in your home. In a flash all is totally silent.

Your heart is beating fast and you are a little out of breath. Your breathing is loud enough to hear until you are relaxed.

You place your ear on your wrist to listen to your pulse and your heartbeat. It reminds you of when you put your ear to a conch and listened to the ocean. It sounds smooth and strong until you pick up the sound of your grumbling stomach. You are hungry. But the sounds of your belly are for another time. You let out a big yawn just as the toilet flushes and the dog chases a squirrel up a tree.

When you have finished reading "The Inner Ear: Part 1," have everyone sit quietly for a while. Follow the silence with a discussion of what each student remembered and heard during the visualization to break the ice and get students into the visual-auditory mode. Break into groups of no more than three to brainstorm a list of sounds that might be good ingredients in the students' own inner ear creations. You might also want to suggest some sounds to students. Following is a sample list:

an avalanche
a bike coming to a sudden stop
a cat purring
a dog slurping a bowl of water
an eraser removing chalk from a chalkboard
a foot tapping nervously on linoleum
a gargling of mouthwash by a five-year-old
a howl of a coyote
an ice cube tray being loosened up
a jeep spinning its wheels in the mud
a kiss
a laugh coming from a child being tickled
a monkey screaming
a nest of chirping baby birds
an owl hooting in pitch black darkness
a punching bag being whacked
a quart of milk being poured
a rag full of dust being snapped in the air
a stick being snapped in half
a target being struck by an arrow
a ukelele being strummed
a violin humming
a waterfall
an extra two or three jelly beans sliding onto the floor
a yell from an umpire, "You're out!"
a zebra sneezing

After the group comes up with a list of sounds, many wonderful possibilities might follow:

1. Read the list to the class while students have their eyes closed. Then poll the class as to which sounds were strongest, sharpest, and clearest.

2. Have each student attempt to make five of the sounds on the list.

3. Ask each student to select ten of the sounds to include in a short story or a sensory essay or poem.

4. Have students read their writing and make the sounds that appear.

Guided Sound with a Focus on Imagery

As with the previous activity, be sure the students are relaxed and receptive to the journey. Then read "The Inner Ear: Part 2."

"The Inner Ear: Part 2"

A bell is ringing so close to your ear that your head vibrates. Diinnnngg, doonnnngg, diinnnnngg, doonnnnngg sounds between your ears as a bee buzzes inside your two hands cupped together. Zzzzzzzzzzzzzzzzzzzzzzzzzzzzzzzzzz, it flies off while crisp, crunchy oak leaves shatter like glass into thousands of pieces, millions of cracking knuckles under your feet.

A voice is yelling just as car tires come screeching to a halt at a red light. Alarms are ringing all through the town while fire trucks emit their high-pitched horns just as a dog barks at a growling bear near a lake full of splashing swimmers. Breaking the sound barrier, a jet speeds through the sky, and a parrot squawks at the morning sun.

A kettle of boiling water is hissing in the kitchen as the doorbell rings and the cat meows and rubs its head on your leg. A coughing child slides across the wooden floor on a sheet of sandpaper and then the silence fills the house like air filling a balloon.

The lawn mower sounds like scissors cutting your hair just behind your ears as a baby cries inside your throat for its mother. A lamb licks your hand full of honey as a key unlocks a door while snow roars in an avalanche just behind your lower back. Cool winds whisper to your knees as owls hoot into the bottoms of your feet.

You scratch an itch on your nose and it sounds like nails across a blackboard as your back is massaged, sending echoes of ocean waves through your bones and putting you to sleep. The old moon groans a bit as she climbs into the night sky inside your dreams, where a coyote howls with a grin on its face and a piano fills the heavens with chords of joy, heartbeats heard inside your head just above your eyes.

"The Inner Ear: Part 2" is filled with sound images. Introduced in the piece are sounds made next to or inside an area of the body, suggesting that the whole body, not just the ear, is a conductor of sound. Connecting sound with the whole body opens up a number of activities that set the stage for a deeper understanding of sound and a broader use of sound across the curriculum. We might say that whole brain–whole body sound could be the basis for reading, writing, math, science, social studies, and integrated skill development. What follows is a list of possibilities that apply to either "The Inner Ear: Part 2," or a derivative of that guided journey.

Reading

Reading is enhanced by paying attention to the body of sound embedded in a book or a story and the sound that plays upon the body of the reader and the listener. If a student were reading "The Inner Ear: Part 2" to herself, you might ask what sound had the strongest impact on her body. Follow with a reading from anything in literature, newspapers, or from the student's own writing. Discuss the presence of sound in the reading and whether or not the sound could be felt in a place in her body other than her ear.

What do all these questions mean? How do they help develop reading skills? What the activity suggests is that reading involves the whole body, the whole brain. In short, we read not only with our eyes but with our ears. By *ears* we mean the whole kinesthetic vibratory system of the body, since imagination re-creates sound patterns all over the body. The body seems to store sound memories everywhere, and the act of reading stimulates the imagination to reproduce these sounds. To do so, the brain uses keys to every part of the body where these sounds are stored. It unlocks the storage areas, releasing the vibration, which travels through our nervous system and helps us understand what we are reading.

Could we also be suggesting the following? Children and teenagers with reading difficulties may be lacking whole-body skills, preventing them from decoding a piece of literature. Until the whole body begins to read, the eyes and the left hemispheric decoding centers remain passive players, unable to process meaning.

What could be done to help provide this missing link in the chain of meaning making for these children? One step could be to have them practice a series of audible imitations before every reading and identify where in their bodies they feel the sounds. You could work from a master list or make a list of sounds taken from the material the students will read.

Writing

See "The Inner Ear: Part 1."

Math

Have students create a list of sounds (either from "The Inner Ear: Part 2" or another source) in a style similar to that in "The Twelve Days of Christmas," each of which is preceded by a number of an equation. The students recite the list and sing it. For example, an algebra class might create the following:

> $x + y$ = one alarm clock ringing
>
> $x + y + z$ = two beavers belching
>
> $x + y + z + 2a$ = three crows cackling

The list continues through twelve items. Then you might have students tell what values each letter would need to have to produce what appears to the right of the equal sign. Have each student (or team) present a list with sound effects and even imitations (mimes) or visuals of the animals or objects to the right of the equal sign.

Science

Classify the elements of "The Inner Ear: Part 2" into animal, human, nature, and other. In each category assign research for each sound in that category. End with a paper, a show-and-tell demonstration, or a skit.

Social Studies

Explore which sounds are pleasing and which are not. Discuss the role sounds play in our lives. Which ones bring members of a culture together and which tear them apart? Are there sounds we just cannot do without? What you have here is an incredible opportunity to brainstorm an encyclopedia of sounds, to categorize these sounds, to analyze the social functions of sound, and to develop ideas for the creation of sounds that are useful to society.

Integrated Skill Development

There is no skill that "The Inner Ear" visualizations cannot be used to develop. Obviously, listening itself is at the core of experience. Speaking follows, as students attempt to mimic the sounds from "The Inner Ear" experience. Such mimicry requires a keen hearing of students' own speech, which leads to a deeper appreciation of their identities, since students can hear their own lives in their voices. Writing attempts to capture the imagery and sound of life, to place sound in its larger context so that sound and its context are seen as wedded to each other. With listening, speaking, and writing as the basis of skill development, we move into literal and symbolic knowledge, facts/data, and understanding/meaning making. All are set in motion by sound, the inner experience of words, which suggests what the inner auditory memory has already carefully stored and creatively linked together, waiting for the suggestion to play itself out in the conscious lives of students.

When Sound Asks Us to Stand Up and Listen

For a moment imagine you are standing in front of someone who is directing his chanting voice like an invisible paint brush, applying the satinlike finish of sound from your forehead slowly down your face, chest, abdomen, and legs to your feet. You are told that this person is assessing your health through the quality of sound-wave feedback (echo). Your body is alive with the sound of music, some harmonious, some not so.

What if the very sound of your friend's voice contained qualities that revealed information about his psychological as well as physical well-being? What would you say if someone claimed that hidden in the sound of your voice were the psychopolitics of your family, that is, who ruled, who submitted, who repressed, and who truly loved?

Consider this: You speak and the sound you make is picked up by your own skin all over your body as if it were an extension of your ears. Suppose your skin doesn't perform this audio reception very well. If the skin is an extension of the ear, one's hearing would be impaired by skin that was unable to receive the sonic impulses from one's own or another's speech.

A further consideration is that bones are also part of the ear. Suppose that you were deaf, but you hummed. Would you be surprised to find out that, indeed, you heard yourself? Your facial bones and skull pick up the vibration and transmit it to your brain.

Suppose someone suggested to you that you could distinguish generic sounds made by people and objects and that you could distinguish among the sources of these sounds. In a forest of voices, parents and children can often recognize one another's voices. In a forest of chirping, birds can do the same. Following is a list of sound recognition possibilities:

your parents' footsteps
your car's engine
your spouse's cough
the bark of your dog
a familiar guitarist
your baby's cry
water filling your bathtub or the sound of your shower

What if you were told that people who are deaf often hear things when they see them move? For example, a leaf suddenly blown across a pile of leaves and noticed by a person who is deaf will apparently make a noise, but there will be no noise without the accompanying vision of the movement. The same is true of ocean waves, the snapping of twigs, the rushing of water in a brook, the clapping of hands, and the chattering of teeth. The synesthetic connection between the senses either enhances sound for those who hear or stimulates sound for those with hearing disabilities and those who are completely deaf. The program of sounds that fit a category but bear individual characteristics fills our acoustic memory, but no sound programs that memory more potently than the sounds heard in the womb.

The Warble of the Womb

Diane Ackerman notes, "The womb is a snug, familiar landscape, an envelope of rhythmic warmth, and the mother's heartbeat a steady clarion of safety. Do we ever forget that sound? When babies begin talking, their first words are usually the same sound repeated: Mama, Papa, boo-boo. New parents can even buy a small box to set in the crib, which thrub-dubs a recording of a strong, regular heart rhythm at about seventy beats a minute. But if for experimental purposes the boxed heart is set faster than normal, so that it suggests an unhealthy mother or a mother under stress, the baby will become agitated. Mother and child are united by an umbilical cord of sound" (Ackerman 1990, 178–79).

Alfred Tomatis asserts that embryonic hearing takes place much earlier than we think. He cites the case of a young girl whose native language was French but seemed to understand English better than French. It so happened that the mother had a job as an English translator during the first trimester of pregnancy. Tomatis believes this exposure to English accounted for the girl's facility in English (145).

The sonic womb experience must be imitated if it is to be understood as the educational and therapeutic starting point of lifelong learning. Tomatis has developed a tool, the "electronic ear," with gating systems that allow you to hear your current vocal range as well as your true voice range and quality. Gradually the gating system reduces the feedback of the altered voice until your own voice has become patterned after the altered one. At this point you have rediscovered your voice; you are truly able to hear your voice. It is a Tomatis truism that we can reproduce vocally only what we hear. Thus, the electronic ear not only allows you to hear your own voice but to recover your authentic voice. In doing so, your voice recaptures its own ability to charge the brain.

At the heart of the Tomatis analysis of the womb experience and the electronic ear is the concept of "charging the brain." There are sounds (low frequency) that cause the brain to discharge, and there are sounds that cause the brain to become charged with energy. This charging of the brain influences body posture and overall somatic readiness to learn. Tomatis (1991) states, "One of the functions of the ear is to stimulate the cortex to give it the means of animating the body and then spirit for which it is responsible. High frequency sounds, transmitted harmoniously, help do this. Among the hundreds of pieces of music tested over 25 years, we selected and retained works by Mozart and Gregorian Chants" (150).

In the idyllic world of the womb, Mozart and Gregorian chant would not seem as strangers. They are not alone in their capacity to feed the brain what it needs to enter the paradoxical state of rest and readiness. It is Tomatis's assertion that we spend our whole lives listening to and listening for this primal sound as if it were the ideal context in which to learn and make connection, the basic skill necessary for lifelong learning. Tomatis says, "The technique of listening [reference is to what his electronic ear does] is to achieve again this conduction [2,000 cycles per second processed through the bones of the inner ear], which is precisely that of the fetus. All our life we try to re-create this primal audition" (Campbell 1991, 22). As far as reshaping education is concerned, sound and primal music that are compatible with our nature are essential.

Sound, Learning, and the Musical Connection

Diane Ackerman (1990) gives us a sobering story of a public school in New York City. Some classrooms were located on the side of the school that was beside the elevated railroad tracks. By sixth grade, students who had classes in that wing were eleven months behind in reading. When the train track noises were later muffled, the children's reading returned to normal levels (187).

A good education is one that not only eliminates distracting noise, but also uses sound and music that both relaxes and raises attentiveness.

Howard Gardner asserts that *music* is a distinct intelligence.

It is an intelligence we all possess both as listeners and players. We have a penchant for blowing into things as well as banging on things to make sound, to make music. "Although every culture on our planet makes music, each culture seems to invent drums and flutes before anything else. Something about the idea of breath of wind entering a piece of wood and filling it roundly with a vital cry—a sound—has captivated us for a millennia" (Ackerman 1990, 224–25). Every classroom ought to be equipped with drums and flutes not only as curriculum aids but also as natural outlets for energy and emotion.

Don Campbell (1989) tells us, "Music, rhythm, pulse and breathtone can integrate the parts of the brain efficiently, non-invasively, and quickly. Tonal vibration can instantaneously modify breath, blood flow, emotion and cognition. Inner music can synchronize thinking, feeling and physical states . . . Music can physically and emotionally bring diverse systems of body/mind patterns into a harmonic balance" (51).

Tomatis (1991) asserts that music and sound are essential to the development of the body, learning, listening, memorizing, expressing, and communicating. He also points out that a teacher's voice can either energize or tire students. Paying attention to sound and music have been either taken for granted or conceived of as part of a frill aspect of teaching and learning (220–21). The capacity to hear the sound of music is so important that Helen Keller said that deafness was worse than blindness (Ackerman 1990, 192).

Music and sound are used to communicate with people in comas, children who have disabilities, children who have autism and learning disabilities, individuals who are sedentary, people who have angina, people with cancer, the elderly, people with emotional disturbances and mental illnesses, people who stutter, people who have poor images of their own bodies, and people with general patterns of lethargy.

Music is an important way to reduce stress, which interferes with learning. "When music and relaxation are combined, students become relaxed and learn better (Guzzeta 1991, 157). Marcy Marsh (1993) tells us that "growing numbers of educators are exploring new methods for creating heightened learning states. Using the many tools of Accelerated Learning and holistic education—music being a key element—teachers and trainers are creating the very best environment for their students and trainees to learn, to relax, and to enjoy" (197).

The Lind Lists: A Resource Guide and Journal (1993) is doubtless the foremost resource for teachers who want to incorporate sound and music into their curriculum as well as into the cultures of their classrooms. For a copy of this premier resource write to The Lind Institute, P.O. Box 14487, San Francisco, CA 94114. Call 415-864-3396 or FAX 415-864-1742.

Sound and Music as a Framework

When we think of using sound and music as a framework for our classrooms, we mean that when students think of our classrooms, they immediately associate sound and music with it as a place or a space. This association generates a level of expectancy and motivation in students.

The classroom exudes sound and music and therefore, life. It is a place where the air is filled with sound that relaxes, cajoles, energizes, and immediately draws attention. Learning is identified with a space that is shot through with the balm of aural stimulation. Learning is automatically understood to somehow have a connection with sound and music even before this connection is consciously explained and analyzed.

Every teacher should acquire a collection of tapes and CDs. Part of your planning will involve deciding what sounds to start the day with and what sounds to fill and end the day with. In time you learn what to play and when to play it. Chris Brewer's wonderful book *Freedom to Fly* (1993) lists the following effects of music in the classroom and includes recommended musical/sound selections:

> *created a relaxed atmosphere*
> *increased attention*
> *released tension*
> *enhanced imagery activities*
> *aligned groups*
> *created rapport*
> *provided inspiration*
> *added an element of fun*

established a positive learning state
provided a multisensory learning experience that improves memory
created a background sound that focuses concentration
accentuated theme-oriented units

By designing your classroom with a musical/sound dimension, you are also adding an interdisciplinary motif to the aural framework of your class. The various sounds and instruments, chants and drumbeats, tones and timbres, and lyrics cross cultures and suggest to your students that the world of music and sound is far greater than they had imagined. This framework can be an education unto itself.

Setting up the music/sound framework for a classroom often involves spending money apart from the school budget unless your school has advanced to the level of whole-brain awareness, in which music and art are not frills but are as essential as "the basics." Whether you buy your own equipment or sign it out from a media center, it should be a permanent fixture in your classroom.

When your students realize how seriously you take the sound environment, you will have to deal with their itchy fingers and their requests to play their own music. Set clear policies. Sometimes a hands-off approach is best until you feel comfortable with the sound that you integrate into your curriculum. Before you play your students' music, you'll want to become very familiar with the kinds of sounds that recharge the brain and help it work at its optimum.

Crocodile Rocks with Peach Pit Symphonies

Croc is fast asleep on the shoreline of a pond that borders a forest. Beavers have been working the site for ten years and what was formerly a marshland has become a pond where one can canoe, fish, and ice skate in the winter.

It is early November. Croc and Peach Pit have been working so hard the past months that it is time for some relaxation, time to recharge the batteries that are run down.

"You ought to take a rest, Croc. Your eyes have lost their sparkle," says a concerned Peach Pit. Croc knows his best friend is right. One can get so wound up that nature itself seems like a lost memory.

"I'll fly us to the pond you always loved. Spend some time there. Take in the Crocodile Rocks and my Peach Pit Symphonies. It will fill your soul. Maybe you'll be lucky enough to hear the sound of wings!" With that, the pair soars into the sky toward a destination that will change Croc forever.

It isn't easy, but Croc decides to lie on his back, facing the sun as it rises against the trees. He closes his eyes. Peach Pit simply sleeps near his buddy. Soon the auditory landscape massages Croc's spirit. And, for the first time in his life, he hears the sound of wings. At first it is a sudden whoosh, whoosh, whoosh, but as it draws his awareness closer to what it really is, Croc hears breathing, a quick exhaling, and he understands something he never could quite gather into his conscious mind—that the breath of life permeates the universe and can be heard everywhere; each aspect of nature holds the secret of this breath until you are in the right place at the right time and it is revealed to you.

It takes Croc's exhaustion and the letting go into the natural world to open him up to the breath of the world, the utter sound of life. With his eyes closed, heart beating peacefully, and deep trancelike respiration engulfing his own breath, Croc hears the crows, the ducks, and the hawks all swimming through the sky over his sleeping body and speaking to him of the breath of flight, the wind under their wings, the sound of an exhaling he would never forget. This sound, this gift, is as if the winged ones were bringing him back to life with their own breath, their own wings pushing vital air his way.

Near ground level, a gentle wind tosses a few oak leaves around close to Croc's ears. He hears them for the first time, the famous "rustling of leaves." The sound is not ordinary, not the sound he takes so much for granted. It is the same sound, but it is the first time he really hears it. The leaves dart and stop and he hears every acceleration of their movement and every deceleration into emptiness. It is like a constant birth and death, one indistinguishable from the other. He hears the oneness of the world in the simple play of leaves. And he lies there content, with Peach Pit occasionally waking him up to see if his friend is okay.

The branches of trees stretched by the force of an occasional breeze are audibly clear as is the breeze itself. Croc listens to the symphony of trees, whose limbs, plucked by the wind, play a peaceful lullaby that soothes his sleep. They are violins of the softest timbre and such crystalline acoustics and perfect pitch that he smiles, showing his enormous teeth to the blue sky, which hardly notices them, for it is the smile that counts, and the sky shares its breath with Croc and blows across his face. He hears it whisper his name and he is glad.

In the pond two beavers swim to opposite shores. They each find trees they have been gnawing. Croc is aware of the closeness of their chomping. From the depths of his sleep he concentrates on the rhythmic scraping of beaver teeth against tree flesh in such a precise mastication at the service of these great pond planners and architects that he hears them as if they were in his own head. A tree begins to fall and for a minute he is worried, but he has let go of all fear as the treetop brushes his face and settles with a whomp. He doesn't move. The beaver comes up along the side of the downed birch until it is right upon Croc. Croc lies motionless. The beaver moves to his snout and sniffs. Croc feels like laughing but holds it in. The dragging of the beaver's tail to and from his prone body, the sniffing against his cheek, the soft splash as the beaver reenters the pond, and the still vibrating tree next to his ear are the highest quality sounds he has ever heard, all wrapped into one movement of which the felled tree is but a piece.

The sun crosses the pond as it crossed his face and edges over the treetops on the side where he is sleeping. The air becomes chilly and Croc awakes.

"It was beautiful, Peach!" Croc says to his friend, who awoke when the tree fell.

"Did you hear the symphony, Croc?" inquires Peach Pit.

"Oh, Peach, I did, I did. But more than that, buddy, I heard life as it is. I'm refreshed, recharged. I feel reborn!" responds Croc as he stares across the pond at the beaver still working on a tall oak. "There is so much to hear that we take for granted, so much to listen to that will help us understand, so much beautiful sound, such big medicine for the soul, such a big charge for the brain, such life! Life to life, Peach, life to life."

For the rest of the day Croc sits listening and only then does everything he was taught become intelligence.

6

The Moving Mind and the Tactile Brain

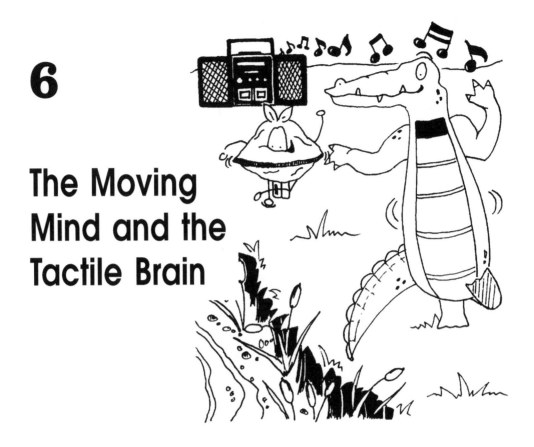

The cosmos can be seen as an infinite dissipative structure which somehow feeds off the far-from equilibrium state itself. In such a model life is no longer seen as an isolated phenomenon briefly flaring up in what otherwise is a dying, entropy filled universe, but as part of a living organism. Dissipative structures live or occur by allowing matter and energy to flow through them like the vortex in a stream of water. In this new vision the Infinite Endless Livingness is viewed as flowing through everything, which is also "Itself." Man is both the flow and the flower, observer and observed, a wave within an infinite ocean. The cosmos begins to look more like an elaborate artwork as we live and flow as an ever transmuting order of creativity.

—Yatri

Yes, the flow. Movement may be the one thing that still rattles many a teacher's cage. Observe the number of times students are told to stop moving. Observe the static quality of classrooms, the age-old image of students seatbound. Yet, everything is in the flow!

Is it accidental that the brain sits within a skull that sits on a neck that sits on shoulders that sit on an upper body that sits on legs that move? The brain is a satellite in motion, both the cause and the caused, the mover and the thing moved.

Was it the act of reading that generated the image of the state of rest that we connect to learning? Was it the notion of the holy man seated in a lotus position and meditating on the cosmos that made us associate wisdom with a state of nonmovement? Of course, both images are connected to quiet moments that are essential to learning, but without the complement of motion, the body and the brain become abstractions that lose sources of information and important forms of communication.

The notion that motion is basic to learning is, of course, underscored by Howard Gardner's including *kinesthetic* among his seven intelligences and why I, in *Doorways to Learning*, list motion as one of the seven major arenas of knowledge. We share commonsensical ideas about motion, such as that walks in the park or on a beach stimulate great thought and insights, even those famous "aha" moments. We know that many scholars and politicians have walking conversations and debates that are far from peripheral to their professions. We know that philosophers such as Socrates and Plato participated in peripatetic dialogues with their students. Finally, isn't it quite remarkable how so many teachers have to move around while lecturing or carrying out what they have planned for their students? Motion must be an important key to learning, one that is a stumbling block to the order and rigidity that schools and classrooms have established as signs of good discipline, good behavior, time on task, and learning; one that educators desperately struggle with, to find out just how to capture the energy of motion and harness it for learning.

We know that there are substantial connections in the brain between areas that control movement, equilibrium, and balance and areas that deal with higher-order thinking and emotion. Jay Seitz (1993) tells us that consciousness may be defined by bodily contact with the world and that the logic, thinking, and emotion of children are rooted in their physical experience (50–55). We might say that intelligence, if defined as the ability to understand what anything is all about, depends on where our bodies are at any given moment. The flow, of which our bodies become part, affects our thoughts.

Even imagining our bodies in motion can approximate our actually doing something. With legs paralyzed, Franklin D. Roosevelt used to fall asleep by imagining himself sledding down a hill and walking back up the hill, sled in hand, over and over again. His imagination compensated for motor activity by conjuring it. Because this process can be very effective, you might want to try a visualization activity such as the following with your students. Begin with a relaxation exercise, then enter into the journey.

Aerobic Visualization

Imagine yourself in the middle of a gymnasium, standing at the center of the basketball court. The floor is highly polished and painted in your favorite colors. Under your feet is a white mat, about two or three inches deep, that will absorb the impact of your feet.

Stand straight. Now bend your knees 'til your rear is almost touching the floor. Propel yourself up off the floor until your feet are one foot off the ground. Stop. With every count from 1 to 10, jump a little higher until by 10 your hair is just touching the roof of the gym. 1 . . . 2 . . . 3 . . . 4 . . . 5 . . . 6 . . . 7 . . . 8 . . . 9 . . . 10 . . . Stop and get your breath.

Imagine yourself anticipating a jog around the gym. The jog will become a run and the run will become a race and the race will become a blur as you enter a new dimension of speed. At the count of 1 begin your jog. As the count increases, gradually speed up so that by 10 you are a blur circling the gym.

1 . . . (Begin your jog.) 2 . . . 3 . . . 4 . . . (By now you should be running.) 5 . . . 6 . . . 7 . . . (At this point you are racing.) 8 . . . 9 . . . (Get ready to become a blur.) 10 . . . (You are now a blur circling the gym in another dimension of speed.) Now the count will go backward so that by 1 you are standing still in the middle of the basketball court.

10 . . . 9 . . . 8 . . . 7 . . . 6 . . . 5 . . . 4 . . . 3 . . . 2 . . . (You are approaching your spot on the mat.) 1 . . . (You are standing still on the mat.) How does it feel?

Correctly done, students will clearly feel this visualization in the whole body (reinforcing another dimension of the mind-body connection). Students may follow up the visualization with a discussion about *memories of movements.* They can converse about activities they've undertaken in P.E. or elsewhere that really got their heart and breath going, that got their energy level up, and that made them feel good about themselves when they finished.

Seitz (1993) notes, "Our brain doesn't simply manage or regulate the body in the way that a chief executive manages a corporation. The brain doesn't direct the body and the body follows slavishly. What the brain communicates to the body depends on what information the body has imparted to the brain and vice versa. The two are in an indissoluble union. The implication is that we literally think with our bodies, that is, we think kinesically" (52). Seitz lists the following as good examples of kinesic thinking: dancing, playing musical instruments, gesturing with the hands, using body language, using vocal intonations, making facial movements, making rhythmic body movements, drawing, touching. This list provides an excellent starting point for constructive classroom activities that integrate body and mind across the curriculum. Charlene C. Wenc (1986) from the American Institute of Adlerian Studies has a wonderful little booklet geared for elementary (but easily translatable for secondary) use. In *Cooperation: Learning through Laughter,* she offers forty-five activities that incorporate a great deal of movement and that foster learning and group consolidation. The following activities, not unlike some in Wenc's book, flow from the idea that touch and movement are a fundamental part of intellectual development.

Dancing and Circle Movement

To begin I must describe how one of my former students integrated dance with reading. Our class had finished James Hilton's *Lost Horizon,* a classic novel about a hidden paradise called Shangri-La. In the novel a group is kidnapped and taken to Shangri-La, where they are exposed to a contemplative life of harmony and peace. Eventually the group has to decide whether to stay or leave. The novel concludes with their decision to depart.

My student decided to create a dance interpretation of the novel. She integrated martial art movements with ballet. Her dance was divided into three parts that corresponded to three stages of the novel. Part 1 interpreted the kidnapping. Part 2 interpreted the time of integration into the peace and harmony of Shangri-La. Part 3 interpreted the act of leaving. She introduced the dance with a five-hundred-word essay describing what she was about to perform. When she was finished, the class was dead silent for what seemed an eternity. Everyone was transfixed by what she had done. Then the class burst into loud applause.

Most students won't choose dance as a means of interpreting material from a particular discipline, but some will. There are ways to use dance so that all will participate.

I have found that organizing my class in a circle not only helps discussion but also makes it easier to incorporate movement into the class. Following is a list of movement activities that could begin a class or punctuate moments to shake things up and bring new energy into the cerebral work that the class is doing:

- Play musical chairs.

- Hold hands; raise and lower them together to the beat of background music. Add head movement and bend the knees, and you've created a linked circle of students who are getting into the beat and forming, as it were, one dancing body.

- Do the same as the above, but let one or two people into the middle of the circle to dance freely.

- Do the same as the above, but the students in the center play "Simon Says" to the beat of the music; for example, "Simon says, 'Stick out your elbows and flap them up and down like a bird to the beat of the music.'"

Playing Musical Instruments

Playing musical instruments may seem obliquely related to movement, but more difficult to incorporate with what students are doing in core subjects such as math, science, English, and social studies. As with all sensory activities, the decision to play musical instruments is a matter of perspective and relates to borders that one builds around and between subject areas. Teachers who conceptually define subjects as fundamentally permeable and interpenetrable have no problems immediately seeing that the suggestion to play musical instruments is a terrific idea to incorporate into whatever they are doing. Following are some ideas:

- ◆ Line up and assign each student a musical instrument. Ask each to pretend to play the assigned instrument by imitating its sound. When all have finished, tell them that they are going to march while playing the individual instruments.

- ◆ Do the same as above, except have the students choose their own instruments.

- ◆ Using objects, such as utensils, pieces of wood, paper, whistles, aluminum pie pans, begin the march. Have students play their instruments to a beat.

Hand Gesturing/Body Language

Most kinesthetic activities have a theatrical quality to them. They require motion and emotion in order to discover and communicate an idea or a feeling. The classroom is, after all, a stage where people of all ages enter the drama of learning in all its rhythms and waves of cognition, emotion, motion, and discovery. The classroom is already a theater, so when we more consciously introduce theatrics into the setting and flow of what we are doing, we are only accenting something that is there in the first place.

Viola Spolin (1986) tells us in *Theatre Games for the Classroom* that "theatre game workshops are useful in improving students' ability to communicate through speech and writing and in nonverbal ways as well. They are energy sources helping students develop skills in concentration, problem solving, and group interaction" (2). Ms. Spolin's book is an excellent source for learning about the sensory, perceptual, and dramatic modes and games that can be incorporated into any classroom. Following are a few ideas based on gesture and body language you will find echoed in her book as well as the books of many others who know the importance of movement in education:

- ◆ Invite one student to the center of the class circle and practice mirroring movements. In this simple exercise, students pretend to be the mirror, copying as closely as possible the movements of the student in the center. A good starting point is the face—moving the mouth, the eyes/eyebrows, the forehead, the cheeks, the ears, the tongue, and the whole head. You can follow this with making faces into the "mirror." After the head, students move down to the shoulders and arms. Walk away from the mirror. This last action will create some fun and laughter as the mirror tries to catch up.

◆ Ask students to close their eyes and to sense the space around them. Ask them to imagine the space making contact with them slowly from head to foot. Reverse your request and ask them to imagine they are making the contact. Continue the awareness by asking that they stretch toward the ceiling, still attempting to imagine the space around their stretched out limbs.

◆ Building on the previous activity, divide the class into dyads or triads and have each group create a dance in which they carve the air with their bodies. Be sure that they consciously decide what kind of motions they will use to carve the air. Have the class try to guess each item being carved in the air. Ideas include cars, bridges, houses, beach scenes, forests, a dinner table that is being set.

◆ This activity has three stages. Students do it individually. Have the student first close the eyes, then take five steps and stop, then turn around, quickly open the eyes, and say something in a loud voice.

◆ Basically, do the previous activity but have two students start off in opposite directions and attempt to stay in synch as they walk, turn, and speak.

◆ You may also try the same activity with the whole class at once.

Vocalizing

Oral activity is motion. It is the motion of the mouth, tongue, jaw, chest, diaphragm, and all accompanying body parts. Of course it is also the motion of the air. As we know, sound and vocalizing influence the bones and body posture. The following three activities support the link between voice and whole body movement.

◆ Be a plane. Imitate the sounds of the engine starting up; the plane taxiing prior to takeoff, taking off, flying, approaching to land, landing, and stopping; and the engines turning off. Accompany the vocal imitations by moving across the classroom as if flying.

◆ In teams of five, become a band with invisible musical instruments. Include a drum, a saxophone, a guitar, a trumpet, and a harmonica. Create an arrangement and play. Include solos for each instrument. Be sure each band member mimes the movements required to play each instrument.

◆ This activity requires two people: one a photographer and the other a butterfly. The photographer is eccentric and talks to the butterfly as it flits around. The butterfly talks back to the photographer. Before the photographic shoot, the pair discuss an overall plan for the shoot, including what they might say and where the butterfly will fly. During the shoot, the photographer takes ten pictures and the butterfly briefly freezes as each picture is taken. After the shoot, the photographer presents the ten pictures and gives a brief description about each picture. The butterfly assumes the photographic pose and is free to talk with the audience about the "frame" of reference in the "picture."

Facial Movements

The human face, like so much of the body, is a register and repository of experience and, in time, it takes on a character all its own, even in twins. Bilaterally controlled by the opposite brain hemisphere, each side of the face contains information that is different from the other side and complementary.

Stereotypically, the left side of the face, wired to the right hemisphere, will contain psychic information and material from the unconscious, darker, more introspective and creative self. The right side of the face, wired to the left hemisphere, will reflect a more optimistic and somewhat superficial reflection of the self. The right side of the mouth will tend to be in a grin while the left side will tend more toward a straight line or frown. You can ascertain what the person is truly thinking by studying the middle of the face from the outside of each eye upward to the scalp and downward to the chin.

It would seem that such a rich repository of personal information might be useful in understanding mood, cognition, and motivation. Facial movement is capable of altering all three. Use the following facial movement activities to change the psychological environment related to class work.

◆ You need a good-sized mirror, bigger than a pocket or a hand-held mirror. Place the mirror so that one student can look into the mirror while another hides behind it as the mirror's voice. The student looking into the mirror takes facial movement directions from the student behind the mirror. The student behind the mirror asks the other students about feelings, mood, and mental acuity. The conversation ends with the voice in the mirror asking puzzling questions such as, "You have heard the sound of two hands clapping, but what is the sound of one hand clapping?" The student looking into the mirror responds.

◆ Have students sit with their chins resting in the palms of their hands, elbows on their desks. Using their fingertips, students tap the sides of their faces. Then they raise their cheek bones as high as they can so that their teeth show and their eyes almost close. Have them lift their cheeks again, but have them then drop their raised cheeks suddenly. Finally, ask them to form the biggest smile they can and hold it for ten seconds. End the exercise with a discussion of how they feel. *This is a good warm-up for a test.*

◆ Divide the students into groups of five. One of the five will be the announcer at a ball game or some event that the group can generally relate to. The other four sit like fans at a game. As the announcer describes the action, the fans simply use facial gestures to reflect the meaning of what's going on. Be sure that the group makes clear to the rest of the class what the event is and who the home team is. Halfway through the event, the fans can begin to accompany their facial gestures with some form of vocalization. *This activity is good to use anywhere when a real break is needed during intense class work or discussion.*

Rhythmic Body Movement

Richard Philips (1993) notes, "Dance is an impermanent art recorded in the muscle memory of dancers" (viii). Everyone dances, except most students in classrooms.

Imagine building into a sixth- or tenth-grade lesson plan time for dancing, time for aerobic movement. Imagine the dance being led by a student while "oldies" play in the background. Then imagine other teachers and adults walking near this classroom, peeking in, being asked by the kids to join in, and finally joining in. Theresa Majoy does this activity with her combined fifth and sixth grades. For more details and tips, write her at the Emerson School, Fitzwilliam, NH 03447.

Besides Theresa, there are classroom teachers, K–12, who have begun to tap into the wisdom of the body, the innate need for rhythmic body movement, and the innate connection between movement and learning. At some appropriate moment see if one of the following activities can be used before or even during a test, a written assignment, a project, or a group problem-solving or research assignment. See if the activity makes a difference.

◆ Gather the class in a circle. All students close their eyes. Request that, at the count of three, all students tap their right feet to a 1-2-3-4 beat. When everyone is in synch, have students make their left feet join in. When all are in synch, stop. For a change of pace, ask all to shake their bodies for thirty seconds or so. Return to the structured circle, begin the foot tapping (both feet), and add both hands, tapping the sides of the legs to the same tempo as the feet are tapping. At this point ask students to add other body movements to the beat without giving up the foot and hand tapping. Afterward, you can begin or continue the regular class work while playing relaxing music to help kids turn the new energy into a relaxed, focused place.

◆ Play pieces of four or five songs in which the beats and rhythms change. First allow students to interpret the music with their extended hands. Follow with an interpretation using their heads, arms, torso, legs, and feet. Tell students that when the music stops, they must, too. Have them observe complete silence as they return to their work. In the background, play sounds of nature.

◆ All students close their eyes. (Be sure students are at least an arm's distance from each other.) Ask them to imagine that they are trees in a breeze, at first mild and slow, which is passing through the space where they are rooted. Have them imagine the breeze gradually picking up in intensity so that in thirty or so seconds it carries the force of a hurricane. In order to show this acceleration, they must move their bodies while keeping their feet firmly rooted in the soil. Students increase the wind on their own, keeping their own timing. After they try it once or twice, you can control the wind force by counting from 1 to 30, with 30 being hurricane force. As with the other rhythmic body movements, this exercise is good before, during, or after any intense curricular project.

Drawing

By the time you incorporate drawing into your whole mind–body classroom, you and your students will begin to sense and understand why these activities are so important. The first understanding has to do with the interconnectedness of everything. This interconnection becomes an underlying message even when it is not understood analytically. It is apprehended directly and is as simple as the acceptance of movement as a normal part of the weave of the curriculum—it's natural.

Drawing is another movement activity that can change the pace, energy, and mental framework of what's going on. Following are three activities that activate both brain hemispheres and, like all movement activities, prime the brain for attentiveness and associational thinking, both necessary in higher-order metaphoric and analytic thinking.

◆ Find three types of music with different beats. Give the kids crayons and large pieces of white paper. Eyes closed and crayon to the paper (start with crayon in right hand), students draw on the top half of the paper whatever the music suggests to them. Be sure to play excerpts from each selection. Have students switch hands and draw again on the bottom half of the paper. When students are finished, let them talk about what they did, then end with a thirty-second period of silence before starting or continuing the planned project or regular class activity.

♦ Unroll a piece of paper big enough to cover the blackboard. Halfway through an activity, suddenly stop and hand each student two or three crayons. Give them five minutes to fill the paper with graffiti related to the project and how they feel about it. After five minutes, return to the project. Do this activity several times, including at the end of the project. When the project and graffiti response are complete, discuss the graffiti before discussing the project.

♦ Before a test, have students (using washable ink) draw as much as they can of a beach scene or a favorite scene from nature on the palm of their nonwriting hand. Be sure they work slowly and carefully. Play an appropriate piece of music and allow about ten minutes. At the conclusion of the activity, begin the test. About halfway through the test, stop and have students carefully copy the scene from the palms of their hands onto their test papers (either front or back). Play the same piece of music. This time allow them about five minutes, then return to the test. When the test is finished, ask students if they think the activity helped. If so, tell them that they may choose to repeat a similar activity before and during another test or project.

Touching

In a sense, the skin is an extension of the brain. Galvanic skin response research shows that, when people with no brain damage watch a series of slides in which a violent act is depicted every fifth slide, the skin registers neuronal change as an output and creates neuronal change as an input. When patients who have damage to their frontal lobes are shown the same slide series, they register no galvanic skin response. This lack of response indicates that something neurological is wrong (Damasio 1994, 208–12).

Being held by someone who cares and loves us is a basic need. Because it is now common thinking in holistic education that the affective and cognitive domains are essentially united in one knowing experience, we know that the absence of touch in a person's life can have profound effects on the person's thinking style and the goals to which that person aspires. Most people have heard stories of orphans who, when left untouched, however well fed, died. This example is extreme, but it certainly shows how important touch is to people. Certainly in this day of frequent lawsuits, most teachers can identify with a fear of touching students. Yet we must touch them, for it is the nature of knowing and learning that without healthy affect, no real learning takes place.

By real learning we mean learning that is not only valued in a conscious way, but also that is remembered as a beautiful experience, much like memories of a beautiful sunset. Real learning moves into the whole body-mind person and becomes another medicine that uplifts students for their whole lives.

Teachers must make their own choices about touching students based on the psychopolitics of their teaching situations. Nevertheless, my impressions are that the best teachers are those who, in some small way, make physical contact with their students. Most successful coaches put their arms around their players, pat them on the back, and in moments of triumph hug them. We never hear complaints about this behavior. I see great teachers do the same or find some way to make contact, even if it is a handshake or a high five. Following are three basically safe activities related to the need for touch.

- In the morning before the day's work begins or at the beginning of each class, gather students in a circle. Go around the circle and have each student slap five with your outstretched hand. They do the slapping. Do it a second time and have students say something like "YEAH!" or "HEY!" This ice breaker establishes the affective contact necessary to properly ensoul the task at hand.

- The following is a guided imagery journey that emphasizes the sense of touch and the whole kinesthetic-synesthetic network in students. This visualization is ideal to begin or end a class with. Of course, as with all the exercises described in this book, you may use it as a basis for writing, discussing, creating art, and researching. When your students are relaxed and ready, you may begin the journey. You can read it as is or adapt it to suit your particular needs.

The Touch of Nature

Imagine yourself leaning up against a windowpane with your forehead and the palms of your hand touching the window. It is winter and the window is cold. The snow is falling and you decide to go outside.

Once outside you stick out your tongue to let a snowflake land on it. It feels delightfully cold as the warmth of your tongue melts it. You feel a slight breeze across your cheeks and the snow brushes your nose. You lower your ungloved hand into the snow and pick up enough to form a snowball. The palms of your hands and your fingers get cold and wet. You toss the snowball at a tree.

You walk toward the tree, but before you get there, the season magically turns into summer. The bark of the tree is both smooth and rough to your fingers. You gently kiss the tree and sense it is grateful.

In the tree is a small kitten that is having a difficult time getting down. You help the kitten as it brushes itself against your neck and you are soothed by its soft fur. You put your nose against the soft nose of the kitten and you smile.

Suddenly, someone taps you on your right shoulder from behind. You are a little startled, but it is just the next-door neighbor looking for her lost kitten. As she leaves with the cat you stop to lie down in the soft green grass. The pressure of the ground against your body feels good. All the things that touched you and that you touched made you feel good today. You realize that touch is an important way of knowing things.

Following are more touch exercises:

- Amass a collection of objects with differing degrees of hardness and softness. Arrange them in random order. Blindfold your students and have each do two things: handle the objects and arrange them in order from hardest to softest object. They must create the sequence using touch alone.

- Collect objects with differing textures—fuzzy, smooth, bumpy, and so on. Blindfold students and have them touch the objects. Then orally or in a drawing, they should describe the textures and how they feel about each one.

Croc Talk

"Hey, Peach, I'm gonna take some dance classes and a couple of art lessons. I think I want the touch and feel of pottery and the potter's wheel!" Croc was talking out loud to himself and by habit mentioned Peach's name, though Peach was not around at the time.

"Yeah, Peach, something happens to me when I start dancing. All kinds of things take place in my head, like things get loosened up from all that motion. Just the other day I was getting down to some serious funky music and when it was over, I suddenly understood Einstein. I'm not kidding. Maybe I can't put it into words, but I knew what he was talking about.

"When I was dancing I saw everything around me differently, but when I slowed down and came to a stop, everything else seemed to stop, too. It was like living side by side with another dimension. There was my dimension and there was everything else. Yet by dancing I got to know myself better and the other dimension, too. This couldn't have happened, Peach, if I hadn't boogied, you know!" Croc was completely into his thoughts by now and by the riverbank he began to dance.

"Then I got myself thinking about us, about how close you and me are to each other, how I am used to having you as my own form of transportation, how I just sit on you and get comfy and we just fly to anywhere like we are one thing. I got to thinking how important it is that our bodies rest against each other, how it gives me a sense of safety, security, belonging, and love, and because of that how my brain can think so clearly, so poetically, so silently, so analytically, so compassionately, so incisively, so interdimensionally, so simply, so complexly, so revealingly, so interconnectedly, so logically, so analogically, so carefully, so freely, so understandingly, so immediately able to apprehend and comprehend reality as it is, so intuitively, so artfully, so . . . "

Peach Pit had returned at the beginning of Croc's litany and was moved by how important it was for the two of them to be able to reach out and touch each other. Peach Pit thought for a while and smiled . . . then danced . . . then delivered the most impassioned rendition of Hamlet's soliloquy ever spoken by a Shakespearean actor.

7

Technology and the Reality of the Senses

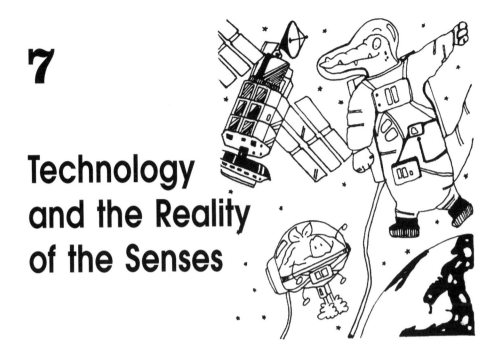

Discussion about computers becomes charged with feelings about what is special about people: their creativity, their sensuality, their pain and pleasure. But paradoxically, when faced with a machine that shows any degree of "intelligence," many of these same people seem pulled toward treating the machine as though it were a person.

—Sherry Turkle

For all the speculative discussion and argument over whether or not computers can or will think like humans, the real question in the unfolding of technology and culture is whether or not the computer can feel. Make no mistake about this. The issue of technology as it impacts culture day to day is not its competition for the primacy of mind but its creeping attempt to become an extension of the senses.

All the arguments about the "thinking computer" are based on false assumptions about human thinking that date back to René Descartes. In the context of ecclesiastical pressure, Descartes negotiated his way to the integrity of individual thought by describing selfhood as the awareness of one's own thinking. In establishing this starting place he managed to dramatize a split between mind and body; thus he allowed the church to retain its moral authority over behavior, what the person-as-body does in everyday life. It was a political sleight-of-hand that allowed Descartes to maintain freedom within the fields of science and math, to pursue the disembodied cogito (or thinking self), and to hand over the world of the senses to the church.

Today the aesthetic, educational, perceptual, and moral realm of the senses has slowly and methodically become the territorial imperative of technology as it competes with religion, philosophy, and theology to lay the groundwork for a sensory revolution. The abstract world of the computer and the evolution of aritificial intelligence (AI) is only a surface manifestation of the deeper reality, the reinvention of the senses.

Western culture is dominated by a strange, paradoxical relationship to the senses, one of extremes. On the one hand there is rejection and distrust of the senses; on the other hand there is glorification and gaudification of the senses. Between these extremes the battle for free speech, educational reform, and the soul of culture is being fought.

Technology is an essential possession of our culture; it must be a carefully crafted tool of the culture of the school. As never before, we need educators who understand what technology is all about as a medium of perception, conception, and expression. To begin to understand this medium so that school can be a safe and sacred place of critical inquiry, applied curiosity, and open communication, teachers must come to terms with the mythology of thinking that technology, taken at face value, tends to perpetuate. It is the myth of the sense-less thought.

It is this abstraction of thought from body, feeling, and emotion as the ultimate definition of thinking that the computer generation would have us internalize, causing us to shrink before its power like an almighty absentee god. This fear of a mighty mind void of sensory delight still controls much of our culture, especially with the images and values propelled currently by extremist ideology masked as religious belief.

Human Thought: The New Realization

The definition of thinking, mind, and reason as separate from sensory experience is so deeply ingrained that we are easily threatened, as educators, by anyone who casts a veil of suspicion over anything in our curriculum that is sensory in nature. Because this threat is a potential travesty, we must be secure in our understanding of what human thinking is really all about.

Most of us live and teach in the framework of developmental psychology, which inversely connects thinking with sensation as a person develops, positing that by a certain time one should be able to think abstractly. Abstract thinking is the apogee of the evolution of thought both individually and communally. Abstract thought is an important development because it frees individuals and cultures from the domination of rigid formations of value and irrational mind-sets driven by ideology. It allows individuals to see through experience to the principles of logic and the conclusions that must necessarily flow from those principles. Yet, as we shall see, even abstract thought is inseparable from material reality and is enmeshed in feeling and emotion.

For many of us the errors of an overly sequential understanding of developmental psychology are based on Piaget's understanding of human cognition or, rather, our misunderstanding of Piaget. Added to this misunderstanding is the popularization of Paul McLean's theory of the triune brain, which stacks the human brain from basic sensation processing through emotional processing to higher-order abstract processing. The model does have a basic truth to it—we do gradually develop higher-order thinking skills over time. But it is an oversimplification of the truth. In fact, it has led to a conceptual framework that is incorrect.

The neurological data we now have point to the control that the limbic system (the mammalian brain in triune brain theory) has in thought processing. "It turns out that the brain's largest and latest development, the cortex, has more inputs from the limbic system than the limbic system has coming from the cortex. **The functional significance of these connections turned out to be the reverse of what we had assumed for decades.** Granted there is a reciprocal relationship between the cortex and the limbic system, each regulating the other, and each ultimately influencing our mental life. But the number and nature of the recursive feedback circuits ensures that the influence of the limbic system is greater" (Cytowic 1993, 161; emphasis in original).

The overly simplified developmental/triune brain model produces an image of discrete, separate functioning over time and space. However, we now know that the brain works analogically, simultaneously, and nonlocally. It's as if we had noticed that when we turn on a switch in one room of a house, all the lights go on in every room to some degree of intensity. In the new model, the lights in the limbic system are even brighter and more intense than we had thought—so bright, in fact, that they light up the whole thinking process itself. Cytowic (1993) reduces this new understanding to five basic points:

1. There is no real hierarchy in brain processing, for the brain processes information nonlinearly.

2. Brain function is not localized in one spot in a one-to-one manner but is distributed throughout the brain; function is distributed and a chunk of brain tissue serves many functions.

3. The cortex contains our model of external reality, but the limbic system determines its relevance.

4. It is an emotional evaluation, not a rational one, that guides our behavior in the long run.

5. Comparisons of the mind to a machine are incomplete because emotion more than reason makes us human (156).

Technology presents us, therefore, with contradictions. On the one hand, it offers a model of thinking that is not in agreement with the latest in neurological research about the role of the limbic system in abstract thought. On the other hand, it attempts to capture the sensory world of young people through interactive video, virtual reality, and the implicit realization that technology gurus subscribe to: **capture their senses, capture their minds.** Let us begin to explore the situation and see what is happening and what educators can do to make sure that technology and the primacy of the senses are truly compatible in the broadest human ethical and educational terms. To start let us look at the phenomenon of the Internet.

Surfing the Internet

To initially grasp the role of technology in education, you need only look up Stephen Bates's cyberspace article "The Next Front in the Book Wars" (1994). In essence the Internet, whose valuable resources are speeding up research projects, written reports, and all other genre of writing, as well as student communication and sharing between and within school systems, has become controversial.

The Internet itself does not self-censor material it makes available. Thus, forces on both sides of the censorship issue have found new turf on which to debate. In fact it is common to find much of the debate right on bulletin boards posted on the Internet. The result of all this disagreement is the possibility that Internet may be banned from schools. An option more in keeping with the commonweal would be either to create a program that limits the access to parts of the Internet or to have students, parents, and administration sign a contract to voluntarily limit access to the Internet for the specific purposes of a school project. Violation of the agreement could result in a retraction of Internet privileges.

What is important here is that technology is bringing the landscape of the world instantly into view, extending the visible world to include the planet in a matter of seconds. The controversy over Internet use in school is basically over access to sensual material: sex, open conversations, and outrageous e-mailers who are nicknamed "flamers."

It is important that the Internet become an essential doorway to information but at the same time not become bogged down in issues of sensory extremes. Schools and parents must have the power to decide what may and may not be accessed on the Internet without becoming partners in censoring and shutting down the access to information.

Technology cannot be conceptualized as a neutral force. Until certain basic controls over the Internet can be created in software form, schools must be vigilant in not allowing the Internet to become anything other than what it is intended to be in the curriculum. As an extension of our ocular sense, it must not be banned but used wisely. A good resource for teachers who want to get online is the January 1995 edition of "Cable in the Classroom," obtainable through local cable companies. The May/June 1994 edition of *Technology and Learning* is also very useful.

But what does all this have to do with "a sensory approach to education"? Before this question can be more substantially addressed, we must dig a little deeper into the emerging technology and its claims on the future of educational experience.

What's Going On in the Schools?

Can we make any general statements about where technology is going in our schools? The following statements may be argued in terms of degree but not in terms of the larger vision.

- ◆ Education is undergoing a technological revolution along with the rest of society.

- ◆ The home-schooling movement is the fastest growing area of school renewal in the United States and, with the emergence of new technology, may become the seedbed of the technological school in the home.

- ◆ All school systems are changing technologically, most too slowly.

- ◆ Teachers will become multimedia experts by the year 2010.

- ◆ Interactive multimedia integration into course content will become a natural development in curriculum planning within schools, among schools in the same system, among school systems, between schools and government, and between home and business.

What Are the Benefits of Technology?

To summarize the coming benefits of multimedia technology in education we turn to Alfred Bork (1992):

- ◆ Active learning based on interaction between the learner and excellent teachers who design the material can occur.

- ◆ Well-developed interactive programs can adjust to the individual styles, knowledge, speed, skills, and desires of the learner, thus individualizing learning.

- ◆ A wide variety of media to assist learning is feasible.

- ◆ New and imaginative roles for teachers are likely.

- ◆ New ways of organizing courses are possible for greater learning.

- ◆ All students can learn to the mastery level (6).

Are Any Schools Living Up to All This?

Let's look at one school district—the Salem, New Hampshire system—that claims to have in place key multimedia elements. These elements are supposed to enable students and teachers to accomplish what Bork suggests will follow from the new technology: "The mission of Salem School District Media Services is to prepare students for the future by providing them with the skills to access and to utilize information in and from multimedia formats" (Crompton 1992, 22). With this mission in mind the district has done the following:

- built a state-of-the-art television studio complex (CTV 30)

- tapped into satellite technology

- created two interactive distance learning classrooms (the classrooms are not in the same school, but they interact through the technology)

- changed from independent media centers that serve only particular schools to a centralized, district-wide media center

- built eight libraries

- provided information access for students via print, audio, video, computer, modem, CD-ROM, and laserdisc

The entire school system centralizes its AV/video software, which is sent daily by courier to whomever requests it. The local cable company provides "Cable in the Classroom." The system is in the process of internally linking learning labs between the junior high and high school so that courses may be team taught between the schools. It goes almost without saying that much teacher training is required to share the possibilities the Salem system opens up.

In Fairfax, Virginia, the public schools go on "Electronic Field Trips," which involve four components:

1. Print materials distributed in advance

2. A pretaped orientation program

3. A live, interactive teleconference with a toll-free call-in number

4. A computer Bulletin Board Service with an 800 number and a voice-based call-in 800 number for schools without the computer-modem set-up (Garcia 1992).

Thayer High School in Winchester, New Hampshire, under the guidance of their nationally recognized principal, Dennis Litky, pioneered a satellite teleconference for teachers and students called "Here, Thayer, Everywhere." The program now emanates from Brown University as "E.G./Math Watch" and is linked with the Annenburg Institute for School Reform.

The Office of Educational Research and Improvement (OERI) has begun a computer link-up with homes, offices, schools, and public libraries where jargon-free information about education and educational resources can be tapped. It is called SMARTLINE (Sources of Materials and Research about Teaching and Learning for Improving Nationwide Education). Information is available through James A. Mitchell, OERI, 555 New Jersey Avenue NW, Washington, DC 20208-5530.

In the Eagan/Dakota Hills District all classrooms have TV/VCRs where they receive programs from "Cable in the Classroom." All TV/VCR units in the school are connected for centralized programming. Students produce a weekly two-hour show about what is happening in school and it goes out to the local community channel. Students broadcast weather and news both to the school and to the community. To find out more about this school contact Eagan High School/Dakota Hills Middle School, 4185 Braddock Trail, Eagan, MN 55123. Call 612-683-6900. Contact persons are Dennis Forman and Cliff Dodge (Garrison 1993).

In Georgia's Carrolton High one social studies class "used the *Video Encyclopedia of the 20th Century* laserdisc, downloading video footage that applied to their project, adding their own music and voice-over and creating their own videos" (Keating 1993, 9). Contact Carrolton High School, 202 Trojan Drive, Carrolton GA 30117. Call 706-834-7726.

Other good sources of commentary and information about technology in schools include two books from Zephyr Press, *Linking through Diversity* and *Creating Context*.

We can get a focused and condensed sense of the potential of technology from assistant principal Helen Horan's (School 10, Perth Amboy, N.J.) remark about the impact of a videodisc system in her school: "Using the videodisc empowers teachers to create lessons which enhance and encourage higher order thinking skills and problem-solving techniques, in addition to being a unique motivational tool which addresses the varied learning styles of our youngsters" (Brady 1994, V8–V9).

As we get closer to understanding the theme of the senses and the horizons of technology in the classroom, let us relate each major point made so far to the central role of the senses.

Access to the Internet and Online Services

Vision and touch are the sensory means of connecting online. Touch a button and watch a screen. Touch and watch. Hand-eye coordination. That's just the beginning. After talking to people who go online, you get the impression that one of the most important virtues one can develop when confronted with online services and information is judgment. There is so much information that one could get lost deciding what to select and what not to. Students need to develop not only fast fingers and eagle eyes, but also judgment about a plethora of information that could get them wired instead of wise. Following is one holistic activity that educators can use to get their students into a healthy frame of mind before going online to retrieve information from educational resources. The focus of this brief activity is twofold: 1. To get students' senses ready for technological interface and 2. To help them become discriminating users of the system. Have students relax, then lead them through this short guided visualization.

Getting Ready to Go Online

Imagine yourself before your computer. Feel your fingertips. Move your eyeballs beneath their eyelids. See yourself turning on the computer and gradually getting into an educational resource through the Internet. Do you know what you are looking for? Do you feel that you will be able to find it without wasting too much time?

Imagine yourself smiling as you explore what is available. Bring a smile to your face. Feel your face smiling. Stretch your fingers and make them dance in the air. Feel good about your eyes and your intelligence. When I count backward from 10 to 1, open your eyes and begin your search.

This kind of visualization humanizes the interface with technology and reminds students of their bodies, feelings, and intelligence. It also makes a point that the technology and the Internet are resources, means to a larger end. This point places technology under another umbrella, a larger, more holistic cover.

Technology and Higher-Order Thinking and Problem Solving

One of the major theses developed in holistic education is that thinking is a weaving of the cognitive and the affective, and that this weave is present in every act of thought, including higher-order thinking and problem solving. The computer and all the software and peripheral multimedia extensions present a model of thinking that is one sided. The computer implicitly teaches that thinking is sequential and analytical, or in its ocular and auditory components it presents the eye and the ear with data that are categorized.

Even when it appears to be oriented to feeling in interactive programs, the computer is not. It has no feeling for what it is doing, whereas students do. The problem of the computer is that it can become more influential than the student who is interacting with it. The student must always give way to the hardware/software world of the computer and become more computerlike, less affective in his or her thinking.

To bring to the forefront the absolute confluence of affective and cognitive, the innate thinking of human beings, teachers and students need to constantly regroup away from the computer to fully recapture what higher-order thinking and problem solving are all about: people interacting with people, people making decisions with people, people succeeding and failing with people—with the computer there as a checkpoint, a database, a theorizing, model-making, scenario-producing, forecasting machine of critical analysis and probability. But always the higher value is not the interaction with technology but technology's potential for improving the interaction between students and teachers and the human sense and feel of things.

Technology as Motivator

Technology motivates in four basic ways:

1. *Immediacy.* Things happen instantly; we live in a society that primes kids for immediacy.

2. *Clarity.* It is not that programs and interactions lack dimensions of guessing and approximations, but as a form it is either on or off. Technology is either totally there for you or not. Once it is on it is your servant.

3. *Power.* Technology gives the user power. It is a servant and you control it. The more you understand, the more you control its potential to be at your beck and call.

4. *Intelligence.* Technology can make you feel intelligent. It fills you with information. You take on its identity even though most of the data are irrelevant or forgotten in a short while.

These four motivational factors are powerful. Teachers could take a cue from them when they think about motivating students. Let us take each of these factors and relate them to the sensory world of students so that technology and its use as a motivational tool are conceptualized in a larger context of what it means to be human.

Immediacy

The senses are constantly tickled by the cultural artifacts that keep society afloat. This tickling is a form of conditioning. What if we surrounded technological interfaces with journaling, artistic expression, and movement? It might look like the following:

1. Before the interface there would be ten minutes of dance and exercise.

2. During the interface students would stop for tea and cookies at a round table and talk about what was happening.

3. After the interface students would add to an ongoing graffiti board.

What we've done with immediacy is ritualized it, slowed it down, connected it to the senses, given it a softer face, and used it to create community.

Clarity

Technology is on or off. But life as a process is simultaneously both and everything in between. To understand this concept, have two kids role-play a computer interface. One plays the computer and one the human. Use your ingenuity to create this scenario, with the goal being the kids' awareness of the sharp contrast between the on-off state of the computer and the much more complex reality of human awareness, feeling, and emotion. End with artwork that expresses the difference.

Power

Power is just a way of labeling the sense of control that is communicated to students via the computer. Of course the computer does not actually communicate this sense; it is a machine designed to transmit control to the user. When the computer user habitually experiences this sense of power, however, he or she develops a sense of expectation in all other relationships that involve the transmission of information.

Most group interactions with computers should be followed by face-to-face debriefings so that this sense of power becomes molded to fit a more human exchange of ideas. There must be a sharing of power among kids; they must feel powerful in a human context and that power must often be defined by cooperation and mutual contribution to a group effort.

There is something to be studied in the way computers provide power. Up to a point it is fine, but we must be wary in a wise and not overly skeptical manner about what is undesirable. The degree can only be gauged when kids are seen working with one another with the computer as an aid in a larger human interchange of ideas and feelings about things.

Intelligence

What is intelligence? Is it information or the things we can do with information, or is it some higher awareness? In fact it is all of these things. The first thing teachers must do when students get information from computers is to challenge them with an "Okay, what now?" Get them to feel the information by putting it to some use, to create something that they care about. Of course data can have some trivial pursuit value, which can be fun and informative and in itself help foster community. In the final analysis we need a shared pool of data to be a culture, but we need people in that culture who know what to do with those data and can determine what is worthy or unworthy of being maintained.

Technology and Learning Styles

Again, we run into the label game. How does the computer deal with learning styles? Is the computer not a learning style itself? How can it deal with the complexity of learning styles? We have thrown the learning style jargon around for years, as if students are nothing but the learning styles we determine they are. Some kids take to computers like others take to water skis. Yet most kids can use computers as well as ski! We cannot label everyone based on rigid descriptions of types. We must avoid the "Oh, this kid's a left-brained sequential type, perfect for this or that!"

The proliferation of computer labs as dumping grounds for all kinds of students is one of the silent tragedies in education at the present time. Use of the computer must be justified, so we throw bodies at them to become "remedialized" in weeks for deficiencies of years. No, technology is a style of learning and it should not be confused with a panacea for addressing the very complex issue of a learning style, which includes not only sensing where a student is coming from but avoiding, at all costs, any labeling response to what we find. Kids need to be encouraged, not stamped with a particular learning style and pushed in front of a computer with its own learning style program.

Full Circle with Croc and Peach Pit

Croc and Peach are in orbit around the Earth like a satellite. They are good for nothing as far as communication devices are concerned. Both feel foolish just circling the planet with nothing of any importance to relay back to Earth.

"Hey, Peach, I have an idea! Let's hop onto one of those satellites and cut in on some conversation. Never can tell what we'll get into, maybe an online conversation through the Internet!"

Peach isn't too thrilled, since outer space is nippy, but he consents. They spot a satellite and propel themselves aboard.

"Great, a computer hook-up. Heavens, the Internet! We're in luck, Peach, in luck!" Peach is used to Croc's hyperbole and just does his patient best.

"The kids will never want to go to a regular classroom again when we fit them out with cybersuits and virtual headgear. Schools will die unless they go full-tilt technology." The voice comes through the Internet. Croc feels his temperature rise.

"What bozo said that!" Croc blows through the satellite system.

"Hey, who is that?" bellows the first voice.

"It's me, Croc, Croc of the heavens above, and I tell you that you are twisted in your understanding of what education is all about. Your cyberspace suit and virtual glasses are okay, but they are amusement park ideas—no imagination but what is supplied. We have an inner sense, the mind's own creative eye and ear and everything else that you guys are trying to shut down. Watch a kid read a book about lions and tigers and you'll understand that cyberspace suits and virtual reality are only one form among many forms. You people who talk revolution in education because of the technological breakthroughs that mesmerize you, you must remember that it's your own imaginations that got you there in the first place!" Croc is heated up.

"Let your space gear come tenth. Let them be told stories about the lion. Let them read about the lion. Let them see pictures of the lion. Let them feel the lion with their own hands. Let them draw the lion. Let them growl like the lion. Let them walk like the lion. Let them cooperate like the lion. Let them walk a path alone like a lion. When that is done, put the gear on them. You may find they are disappointed or that your technopop is taken in its place: not the panacea you thought it was, just another nice addition to things."

There is no further communication along the Internet. But, as is often Peach Pit's habit, he just smiles at Croc's emanations of wisdom.

8

Sensory Learning and Spirituality in Children

Children try to understand not only what is happening to them, but why; and in doing that, they call upon the religious life they have experienced, the spiritual values they have received, as well as other sources of potential explanation.

—Robert Coles

For whatever reason, we tend to be skeptical when we raise the issue of spirituality. In reference to children we seem more tolerant, give spirituality more credence, because we associate it with innocence and trust, which may be washed away with age and experience. We see childhood as a time of play, finger paints, cuteness, exploration, and love.

We define a child as a sensory being who has to be carefully watched, for who knows where those hands, arms, legs, eyes, and ears will take the little one? The spiritual life of children is intrinsically connected to what we observe about them, their sensory life, their effervescence. In an ideal world this life would unfold in a marriage of harmonious balance where body and spirit are not at war with each other, where schools have miraculously united the two so that the sensory life of children and teenagers is seen as an essential manifestation of their spirits, of their spiritual life. It is of such importance that it is not to be stamped out by a moral ethic that transforms pedagogy into an act of mind separated from body. When this separation occurs in either the home or the school, the mental life of children follows a particular path.

As Robert Coles (1990) notes,

> As I go over the interviews I've done with children, I find certain psychological themes recurring. I hear children [on tape] talking about their desires, their ambition, their hopes and also their worries, their fears, their moments of deep and terrible despair — all connected in idiosyncratic ways, sometimes, with Biblical stories, or with religiously sanctioned notions of right and wrong or with rituals such as prayer and meditation. Indeed the entire range of children's mental life can and does connect with their religious and spiritual thinking. Moral attitudes, including emotions such as shame and guilt, are a major psychological and sometimes psychiatric side of young spirituality (108).

Usually the shame and guilt arise from some repression of sensual life—a repression of bodily movement, a lack of touch and affection, even a lack of the touch of a tender voice, or doubts and difficulties surrounding the sexual coming of age. As Coles states, all these forms of repression influence the mental lives of children because they affect spiritual life, which in turn influences what and how children learn or don't learn.

What kind of student can the young man who wrote the following essay be? The assignment was to focus on three memories and use a traditional essay format, which I modify and call "First Paragraph Design."

I Remember

I remember three things from my past. The first thing I remember is that I'm adopted. The second thing I remember is my family. Lastly, I remember that life isn't all people say it is.

I'm adopted because my mom didn't want to take care of me. My mom was 16 when I was born. My grandparents ended up adopting me at birth.

I'll always remember my family. They weren't always there when I needed help but they were there enough. My family is all I need until I'm out of the house.

Life isn't what everybody thinks it is, for example the police are always blaming me for something. It's hard to cope with some things from my past but I don't even think about some of it. Life isn't the greatest in _____.

In conclusion I can say that I'm different from all other people. I don't like talking about my past and I don't want to. That's all I have to say because I don't want to think.

This essay ends on a most telling note—"I don't want to think." Here is a young man who has had his feelings hurt early in life and who has managed to survive but not really value learning. He really doesn't want to think, not only about his past, but also as a process of being completely human. When your feelings and senses have been abused, it is difficult to learn, since learning and thinking are affective in nature.

It is incumbent upon educators who understand the emphasis this book has placed upon the senses to realize that this emphasis is essentially connected to matters of the spirit; together, the senses and the spirit form one point of view. The repression of the senses and intuitive as well as affective learning has been one of the greatest obstacles to creating schools that are warm and caring and respectful of the myriad ways we all learn.

As Thomas Ray (1994) notes, "School knowledge is explicit and rational and is regarded with greater respect than knowledge that is apprehended affectively or intuitively. Accordingly, students acquire a view of knowledge that places it outside themselves as something to be acquired through academic work and appeal to authority, and they learn to delegitimate and devalue personal and other nonacademic learning experiences" (30). The outer senses, the imaginative senses, the kinesthetic sense, the synesthetic senses permeate every human being. All senses are expressions of the spirit; they are necessary senses if education is to be truly nurturing, encouraging, and advancing of the human spirit.

Croc and Peach Pit's Conversation under the Stars

"Well, Peach, seems like it's time to go. The stars are beautiful now that we're back to Earth!"

"Yea, Croc, it's been an adventure flying through this book. We started out with a big vision of what the senses were all about, to make education truly whole brained, but we didn't stop with the vision. We did the vision. We became all that we saw!"

"It's all for the students, the children, the teens, the teachers, and for a better world for everybody!" says Croc.

"The stars are twinkling like the light from the eyes of youngsters discovering the world with their senses, discovering what it is like to be loved and accepted, nurtured and challenged through the union of body and soul, flesh and spirit, sense and mind," responds Peach.

"It's a long-haul vision and a practice that takes time and a sense of community with other teachers," replies Croc.

"Wow, see that shooting star, Peach, see that shooting star, it dipped into the night right behind you!" says an awestruck Croc.

"Croc?" asks Peach.

"Yeah, Peach?" responds Croc in the same quizzical fashion.

"I love you!"

"You, too, Peach!"

"Hey, climb aboard, Croc, the spirit is moving me, so we gotta go to the desert. There's a beautiful Indian guide there waiting to show us how wonderful life is when the spirit is set free through the senses!"

"Let's go, Peach. Sounds like fun!"

Bibliography

Abbott, Edwin A. 1983. *Flatland.* New York: Barnes and Noble.

Armstrong, Thomas. 1985. *The Radiant Child.* Wheaton, Ill.: Theosophical.

Bates, Stephen. 1994. "The Next Front in the Book Wars." *The New York Times.* November 6: 4A.

Beadle, Muriel. 1971. *A Child's Mind.* New York: Anchor.

Berry, Wendell. 1977. *The Unsettling of America Culture and Agriculture.* New York: Avon.

Bork, Alfred. 1992. Guest Editorial. *The Journal: Technological Horizons in Education.* 20, 5: 6.

Boyd, William, ed. 1967. *The Emile of Jean Jacques Rousseau.* New York: Teachers College Press.

Brady, Holly. 1994. "Stanley Kluz." *Technology and Learning* 14, 18: 6–9.

Brewer, Chris. 1993. *Freedom to Fly: 101 Activities for Building Self-Worth.* Tucson, Ariz.: Zephyr Press.

Brewer, Chris, and Don Campbell. 1991. *Rhythms of Learning.* Tucson, Ariz.: Zephyr Press.

Calkins, Lucy McCormick. 1983. *Lessons from a Child: On the Teaching and Learning of Writing.* Exeter, N.H.: Heinemann Educational Books.

Campbell, Don. 1989. *The Roar of Silence.* Wheaton, Ill.: Theosophical Publishing House.

Cannon, Carl. 1993. "Honey, I Warped the Kids." *Mother Jones* July/August. 95–96.

Casanave, Suki. 1993. "Ten Days on Hog Island." *Yankee Magazine* June: 66–78.

Castaneda, Carlos. 1972. *Journey to Ixtlan: The Lessons of the Don Juan.* New York: Pocket.

Chance, Paul. 1987. "The Me I Didn't Know: Pretending to Be Someone Else as a Way to Self-Improvement." *Psychology Today* 21 (January): 20.

Coles, Robert. 1990. *The Spiritual Life of Children*. Boston: Houghton Mifflin.

Crain, William. 1993. "Technological Time Values and the Assault on Healthy Development." *Holistic Education Review*, 6, 2: 27–34.

Crompton, Marie. 1992. "Bring on the 21st Century! The Salem School District Is Ready." *Tech Trends* 37, 6: 22–24.

Cytowic, Richard E. 1993. *The Man Who Tasted Shapes*. New York: G. P. Putnam.

Damasio, Antonio R. 1994. *Descartes Error: Emotion, Reason and the Human Brain*. New York: G.P. Putnam.

Doherty, Thomas. 1993. "Hollywood: As Technology Breaks Down the Barrier Between Spectator and Spectacle Movies May Become Bigger Dinosaurs." *The Boston Globe*. June 27: 67(10).

Dubos, Rene. 1968. *So Human an Animal*. New York: Scribner's.

Eastman, Valerie J. 1993. "The Effects of Music and Imagery on Learning and Attitudes in an Industry Training Class." *The Journal of the Society for Accelerative Learning and Teaching*. 18, 3.

Fleming, E. McClung. 1991. "The Mens' Movement: Revising Our Paradigm of Masculinity." *Chrysalis* 6, 3: 136–44.

Galyean, Beverly-Collene. 1983. *MindSight*. Long Beach, Calif.: Center for Integrative Learning.

Garcia, Judith M. 1992. "Electronic Field Trips: Real World Encounters in Your Classroom." *The Journal: Technological Horizons in Education* 20, 5: 60–62.

Garrison, Anne. 1993. "The Electronic Classroom." *Cable in the Classroom* February: V8–V9.

Gates, Bill. 1995. *The Road Ahead*. New York: Viking, Penguin.

Gilligan, Carol. 1982. *In a Different Voice*. Cambridge, Mass.: Harvard University Press.

Gravelle, Karen, and Robert Rivlin. 1984. *Deciphering the Senses*. New York: Simon and Schuster.

Greeley, Andrew M. 1993. "Bricolage among the Trash Cans." *Society* 30 (January/February): 70–75.

Healy, Jane M. 1987. *Your Child's Growing Mind*. New York: Doubleday.

Highwater, Jamake. 1981. *The Primal Mind*. New York: New American Library.

Hunt, Morton. 1982. *The Universe Within*. New York: Simon and Schuster.

Jaynes, J. 1977. *The Origin of Consciousness and the Breakdown of the Bi-Cameral Mind*. Boston: Houghton Mifflin.

Jessel, David, and Anne Moir. 1989. *Brain Sex: The Real Differences between Men and Women.* New York: Dell.

Johnson, Robert A. 1983. *We.* New York: Harper and Row.

Jung, Carl G. 1965. *Memories, Dreams, Reflections.* Trans. by Aniela Jaffe. New York: Vintage.

————. 1973. *Mandala Symbolism.* Princeton, N.J.: Princeton University Press.

Keating, Lynn Hoffman. 1993. "The 21st Century School." *Cable in the Classroom* February: V8–V9.

Kohler, Wolfgang. 1971. *The Selected Papers of Wolfgang Kohler.* Edited by Mary Henle. New York: Liveright.

Kranyik, Margery A. 1982. *Starting School: How to Help Your Three-To-Eight Year Old Make the Most of School.* New York: Continuum.

The Lind Lists: A Resource Guide and Journal. 1993. San Francisco: The Lind Institute.

Logan, Jennifer Wilder. 1992. "A Scientist's Reverence for Life." *Chrysalis,* 7, 1: 65–70.

Mellon, Nancy. 1992. *Storytelling and the Art of Imagination.* Rockport, Ma.: Element Books.

Mondo 2000. 1993. Issue #10. Berkeley: Fun City Megamedia.

Murdock, Maureen. 1987. *Spinning Inward.* Boston: Shambhala.

Murphy, Michael. 1992. *The Future of the Body: Explorations into the Further Evolution of the Body.* New York: G.P. Putnam.

Nash, Paul. 1968. *Models of Man.* New York: John Wiley.

Ornstein, Robert, and David Sobel. 1987. *The Healing Brain.* New York: Simon and Schuster.

Paley, Vivian Gussin. 1993. "Review of Barrie Thorne's Book: *Girls and Boys In School.*" *The New York Times* May 16: 43.

Pearce, Joseph Chilton. 1985. *Magical Child Matures.* New York: E.P. Dutton.

Penfield, Wilder. 1975. *The Mystery of Mind: A Critical Study of Consciousness and the Human Brain.* Princeton, N.J.: Princeton University Press.

Perelman, Lewis J. 1992. *Schools Out: Hyperlearning, the New Technology, and the End of Education.* New York: William Morrow.

Philips, Richard. 1993. Introduction. *Alvin Ailey American Dance Theatre Jack Mitchell Photographs.* Kansas City, Mo.: Andrews and McMeel. vii–xii.

Ray, G. Thomas. 1994. "Rational Schooling and the Decontextualized Learner: Moral Perspectives of the Implicit Curricula from a Batesonian Perspective." *Holistic Education Revue* 7, 3: 25–34.

Restak, Richard M. 1979. *The Brain: The Last Frontier.* New York: Warner.

Russell, Peter. 1979. *The Brain Book.* New York: E.P. Dutton.

Seitz, Jay A. 1993. "I Move . . . Therefore I Am." *Psychology Today* 26: 50–56.

Sheikh, A., and Katherina S. Sheikh, eds. 1985. *Imagery in Education.* Farmingdale, N.Y.: Baywood.

Shlain, Leonard. 1991. *Art and Physics: Parallel Visions in Space, Time, and Light.* New York: William Morrow.

Spolin, Viola. 1986. *Theatre Games for the Classroom: A Teacher's Handbook.* Evanston, Ill.: Northwestern University Press.

Steinem, Gloria. 1992. *Revolution from Within.* Boston: Little, Brown.

Steiner, Rudolph. 1976. *Practical Advice to Teachers.* Hudson, N.Y.: Anthroposophic Press.

———. 1978. *A Theory of Knowledge Implicit in Goethe's World Conception.* Spring Valley, N.Y.: Anthroposophic Press.

Stevens, John O. 1971. *Awareness: Exploring, Experimenting, Experiencing.* Moab, Utah: Real People Press.

Talbot, Michael. 1991. *The Holographic Universe.* New York: Harper Collins.

Thorne, Barrie. 1993. *Gender Play: Girls and Boys in School.* New Brunswick, N.J.: Rugers University Press.

Tomatis, Alfred A. 1991. *The Conscious Ear.* Barrytown, N.Y.: Station Hill Press.

Twitty, Anne. 1986. "Seven Long Years." *Parabola* 11, 4: 12–16.

Weeks, Bradford S. 1991. "The Physician, the Ear, and Sacred Music." In *Music: Physician for Times to Come.* Edited by Don Campbell. Wheaton, Ill.: Quest.

Wenc, Charlene. 1986. *Cooperation: Learning through Laughter.* Chicago: American Institute of Adlerian Studies.

Wilbur, Ken. 1980. *The Atman Project: A Transpersonal View of Human Development.* Wheaton, Ill.: Theosophical.

Williams, Linda Verlee. 1983. *Teaching for the Two-Sided Mind.* New York: Simon and Schuster.

Williams, Strephon Kaplan. 1980. *Jungian-Senoi Dreamwork Manual.* Berkeley: Journey Press.

Zajonc, Arthur. 1993. *Catching the Light: The Entwined History of Light and Mind.* New York: Bantam.